STUDENT DRAMA SERIES
General Editor: MICHAEL MARLAND, B.A.

BILLY LIAR

047306

BILLY LIAR
A PLAY BY WILLIS HALL and
KEITH WATERHOUSE

EDITED BY MICHAEL MARLAND, B.A.

With a contribution by ALBERT FINNEY
Press reviews by the dramatic critic of *The Times*,
Robert Muller and
W. A. Darlington
Set design by Alan Tagg
Photographs of the London production

Nelson Blackie

Nelson Blackie
Westercleddens Road
Bishopbriggs
Glasgow
G64 2NZ UK

Thomas Nelson and Sons Ltd
Nelson House   Mayfield Road
Walton-on-Thames   Surrey
KT12 5PL   UK

51 York Place
Edinburgh
EH1 3JD   UK

Thomas Nelson (Hong Kong) Ltd
Toppan Building 10/F
22A Westlands Road
Quarry Bay   Hong Kong

Thomas Nelson Australia
102 Dodds Street
South Melbourne
Victoria 3205   Australia

Nelson Canada
1120 Birchmount Road
Scarborough   Ontario
M1K 5G4   Canada

Billy Liar © Waterhall Productions Limited 1960
Novel into Play and Questions © Michael Marland, 1966
Production Note by the Authors © Waterhall Productions Limited 1960

© An Actor's Point of View © Blackie & Son Limited 1966

First published by Blackie and Son Ltd 1966
ISBN 0-216-88911-1

This edition published by Thomas Nelson and Sons Ltd 1993

ISBN 0-17-432475-8
NPN 9 8 7 6 5 4 3 2

All rights reserved. No paragraph of this publication may be reproduced,
copied or transmitted save with written permission or in accordance with
the provisions of the Copyright, Design and Patents Act 1988, or under the
terms of any licence permitting limited copying issued by the Copyright
Licensing Agency, 90 Tottenham Court Road, London W1P 9HE.

Any person who does any unauthorised act in relation to this publication
may be liable to criminal prosecution and civil claims for damages.

Printed in Hong Kong

CONTENTS

ACKNOWLEDGMENTS

The editor is grateful to the following for their help in the preparation of this volume:

Messrs. Michael Joseph Ltd., Mr. Hall and Mr. Waterhouse for permission to reprint *Billy Liar*.

Mr. Albert Finney for his contribution *An Actor's Point of View*.

Mr. Alan Tagg for his drawing of the original set.

Lewis Morley Studios Limited for permission to reproduce the photographs of the first London production of *Billy Liar*.

The Times for permission to reprint from an extract from the review from *The Times* of September 14th, 1960.

Associated Newspapers Ltd. for permission to reprint an extract from the review by Robert Muller from the *Daily Mail* of September 14th, 1960.

The Daily Telegraph and Mr. Darlington for permission to reprint an extract from the review by W. A. Darlington from *The Daily Telegraph* of September 14th, 1960.

Messrs. Michael Joseph and Mr. Waterhouse for permission to include extracts from the novel *Billy Liar* by Keith Waterhouse.

COPYRIGHT NOTE

This play is reprinted by kind permission of the copyright holders.
All rights whatsoever in this play are strictly reserved. Applications for
performance etc. by amateur companies should be made to:

Evans Brothers Limited,
Montague House, Russell Square
London W.C.1

Professional managements, seeking permission to perform this play, should
apply to:

Harvey Unna,
24 Pottery Lane,
Holland Park,
London W11 4LZ

Billy Liar

by Willis Hall and
Keith Waterhouse

THE CHARACTERS

GEOFFREY FISHER

ALICE FISHER, his wife

BILLY FISHER, their son

FLORENCE BOOTHROYD, Alice Fisher's mother

ARTHUR CRABTREE

BARBARA

RITA

LIZ

✳ ✳ ✳
Act 1

THE SET *consists of a living-room, entrance hall and a section of the garden of* GEOFFREY FISHER'S *house. It is a typical lower middle-class detached house in an industrial town in the north of England. To the left of the stage is the garden containing a small garden seat. The entrance to the house from the garden leads directly into the hallway with stairs going up to the bedrooms. Through the hallway is the living-room where most of the action of the play takes place. There is also a door in the living-room* R., *leading into the kitchen. The room is furnished with an uncut moquette three-piece suite and a dining-room suite in dark oak. The furniture is quite new, but in dreadful taste—as are also the plaster ornaments and the wall plaques with which the room is over-dressed. Above the fireplace is the usual collection of family photographs on the mantel-piece and above the mantelpiece is a large brass-studded circular mirror. The room also contains a cheap and flashy cocktail cabinet, a large television set and also a sideboard with two cupboards.*

As the curtain rises we discover FLORENCE BOOTHROYD *sitting on the couch. She is* ALICE FISHER'S *mother, an old lady in her eighties, who finds it impossible to accustom herself to the modern way of life. She continually talks to herself and when she cannot be heard her lips continue to move. She is in the habit of addressing her remarks to inanimate objects. At the moment she is going through the contents of her large handbag. The handbag is open on her knee and as she takes out each object she examines it and then puts it down on the couch beside her, making a neat display. She has already taken out a few odd possessions and, at the moment, she is holding her old-age pension book. She addresses the sideboard.*

1 FLORENCE. I don't know . . . They haven't stamped my book now . . . They haven't sent it up. It should have gone up last week but they haven't sent it up. [*She puts down the pension book and takes a white hospital appointment card from her handbag.*] That's not right, either. Doctor Blakemore? I've never seen Doctor Blakemore. Which is Doctor Blakemore? I bet it's that blackie. Else it's the lady doctor. I'm not seeing her. Tuesday? They know I never go on Tuesdays. I've never been on Tuesday yet. Doctor Thorpe said . . .

It comes to her that she is alone in the room. Putting down the hand-bag she rises and crosses slowly and flat-footed to the sideboard. She attempts to open the right-hand cupboard but, discovering it is locked, returns to the couch and again takes up her handbag.

He's as bad. And she encourages him. He lives in that bed. [*Noting the appointment card on the couch she picks it up.*] And where's that crêpe bandage they were going to get me? [*She puts down the card.*] What's he always keep it locked up for, anyroad? There's neither sense nor reason in that. And she never tells you anything.

ALICE FISHER, GEOFFREY'S *wife, enters from the kitchen. She is a woman in her middle forties. Both* ALICE *and her husband have had working-class upbringings, but* GEOFFREY'S *success as a garage owner has moved them up into this new stratum of society. At the moment* ALICE *is caught up in the normal day-to-day rush of breakfast-time. She is speaking to her husband who is in the kitchen.*

2　ALICE. Well, you do what you think fit, Geoffrey. Do what you like—it's no good me saying anything. But I know what I'd do. He still owes you for that last job you did for him.

ALICE *crosses the room towards the hall, ignoring her mother who speaks to her as she passes.*

3　FLORENCE. Who's Doctor Blakemore? Which one is that, then? Is that the one you went to?

4　ALICE [*entering the hall she calls up the stairs*]. It's time we were having you down, my lad. That bedroom clock's not fast, you know. It's half-past nine turned.

ALICE *turns and re-enters the living-room.*

5　FLORENCE. I'll bet it's that blackie, isn't it? I'll bet it's him.

6　ALICE. Who? Blakemore? Yes, I think it is.

7　FLORENCE. I'm not seeing him. I shan't go. I shall stop at home.

8　ALICE. If they say you've got to see him—you've got to see him, Mother. It's no good arguing. That's all there is to it.

GEOFFREY FISHER *enters from the kitchen. He is a tall man in his early fifties. He is carrying a few invoices and, crossing and seating himself in an armchair, he begins to go through them.*

1 FLORENCE. They caused all that bother on the buses in Birmingham. And Egypt. Mau-Mau. I make no wonder Eden's always so badly. And him upstairs. He's just as bad. I think it's time his father talked to him. I don't know why he puts up with it. I can't understand why he lets him carry on like that.

2 GEOFFREY [*looking up from the invoices he speaks to* ALICE. *In his speech he uses the adjective 'bloody' so frequently that it becomes completely meaningless*]. It's all right you talking, Alice, you don't understand. I've got no bloody choice. I can't turn work away.

3 ALICE. I've said what I've got to say. I'm not saying anything. I'm keeping out of it.

4 FLORENCE. They let him carry on just as he likes. I wouldn't. I'd see to him.

5 GEOFFREY. Where's his bloody lordship, then?

6 FLORENCE. I'd tell her. She lets him lead her on. She wants to go up to him with a wet dish-cloth and wring it over his face. That'll get him up.

7 GEOFFREY. He wants a bloody good hiding.

8 FLORENCE. . . . that'd move him . . .

9 ALICE. I've shouted him three times.

10 FLORENCE. . . . that'd shift him . . .

11 GEOFFREY. It's every morning alike.

12 FLORENCE. . . . he'd have to get up then.

13 GEOFFREY. You let him do just as he likes!

14 ALICE [*takes up the poker and a small shovel from the fireplace and crosses into the hall and calls up the stairs*]. Billy! . . . Billy! [*She bangs the poker against the shovel.*] I shan't tell you again. If I come up there you'll know about it! I suppose you know what time it is! Your boiled egg's stone cold and I'm not cooking another.

15 FLORENCE. She lets him do just as he likes.

1 GEOFFREY. Go up to him. Go up and kick him out. He's
bloody idle!

ALICE *returns into the living-room and places the poker and shovel
back into the fireplace.*

2 ALICE. It's all right you sitting there. You don't stand need to
talk. You haven't emptied them ashes yet.

3 FLORENCE. She wants to go up to him. I would. [*She is now
returning the objects to her handbag and pauses when she comes to the
appointment card.*] It's a mystery to me about that crêpe
bandage. I know I had it. It's in this house somewhere.

4 GEOFFREY. You can't put anything down in this house. Not
without somebody bloody shifting it. And who keeps
taking my invoices out of that vase? Somebody bloody
does.

5 FLORENCE. He ought to see that window's properly locked
every night. He never bolts that back door properly. It
wants doing. There's some more blackies moved in
where Whitakers used to live.

BILLY FISHER *begins to come down the bedroom stairs. He is nineteen
years old and slightly built. He is wearing an old raincoat over his
pyjamas. He is smoking a cigarette.*

6 ALICE. Is that him? He's stirred himself at last, then. I'll see
what his breakfast is doing.

ALICE *goes out to the kichen as* BILLY *reaches the foot of the stairs.*
BILLY *takes the morning paper from behind the door and enters the
living-room.*

7 FLORENCE. She lets him do just as he likes.

8 BILLY [*reading aloud from the paper*]. Cabinet Changes Imminent.

9 GEOFFREY. Yes, and you'll be bloody imminent if you don't
start getting up on a morning.

10 BILLY. Good morning, Father.

11 GEOFFREY. Never mind bloody good mornings. It's bloody
afternoon more like. If you think your mother's got

nothing better to do than go round cooking six break-fasts every morning you've got another think coming.

2 FLORENCE. She lets him do what he wants.

3 BILLY [*ignoring his father he turns and bows, acting out the situation to his grandmother*]. Your servant, ma'am.

4 GEOFFREY. And you stop that bloody game. I'm talking to you. You're bloody hopeless. And you can start getting bloody well dressed before you come down in the morning.

5 FLORENCE. He wants to burn that raincoat. He wants to burn it. Sling it on the fire-back. Then he'll have to get dressed whether or no.

6 BILLY. I gather that he who would burn the raincoat is Father and he who should get dressed of a morning is my good self. Why do you always address all your remarks to the sideboard, Grandmother?

7 GEOFFREY [*almost rising from his chair*]. Here, here, here! Who do you think you're bloody talking to? You're not out with your daft mates now. And what time did you get in last night? If it was night. This bloody morning, more like.

ALICE *enters from the kitchen.*

8 BILLY. I really couldn't say. 'Bout half-past eleven, quarter to twelve. Good morning, Mother.

9 GEOFFREY. More like one o'clock, with your bloody half-past eleven! Well, you can bloody well start coming in of a night-time. I'm not having you gallivanting round at all hours, not at your bloody age.

10 BILLY. Who are you having gallivanting around, then?

11 GEOFFREY. And I'm not having any of your bloody lip. I'll tell you that, for a start.

12 ALICE. What were you doing down at Foley Bottoms at nine o'clock last night?

13 BILLY. Who says I was down at Foley Bottoms?

1　ALICE. Never mind who says, or who doesn't say. That's got
    nothing to do with it. You were there—somebody saw
    you. And it wasn't that Barbara you were with, either.

2　FLORENCE. He wants to make up his mind who he is going
    with.

3　GEOFFREY. He knocks about with too many lasses. He's out
    with a different one every night. He's like a bloody lass
    himself.

4　BILLY. Well, you want to tell whoever saw me to mind their
    own fizzing business.

5　ALICE. It is our business—and don't you be so cheeky. You're
    not old enough for that.

6　FLORENCE. If she's coming for her tea this afternoon she
    wants to tell her. If she doesn't I will.

7　BILLY. I suppose that she who's coming for her tea is Barbara
    and she who wants to tell her is Mother and . . .

8　ALICE. I've told you—shut up. I'm going to tell her, don't
    you fret yourself. You've never played fair with that
    girl. Carrying on. I'm surprised she bothers with you.
    You shouldn't mess her about like that. One and then
    the other. That's no way to carry on. I know where
    you'll finish up—you'll finish up with none of them—
    that's where you'll finish up.

9　GEOFFREY. He'll finish up on his bloody ear-hole. I'm not
    having him staying out half the night. Not at his age.
    He's not old enough. He'll wait till he's twenty-one
    before he starts them bloody tricks. I've told him before,
    he can start coming in of a night or else go and live
    somewhere else.

10　BILLY. Perhaps I will do.

11　ALICE [*ignoring him*]. I can't understand that Barbara—why she
    does bother with you. Are you supposed to be getting
    engaged to her or aren't you?

12　GEOFFREY. He doesn't know who he's bloody getting engaged
    to.

1 FLORENCE. He wants to make his mind up.

2 ALICE [*ignoring* GEOFFREY *and* FLORENCE]. Because she's not like
these others, you know. That time I saw you in the
arcade with her she looked respectable to me. Not like
that Liz or whatever her name is. That scruffy one you
reckoned to be going with. Her in that mucky skirt. Do
you ever see anything of her still?

3 GEOFFREY. He sees so many bloody lasses he doesn't know
who he does see.

4 FLORENCE. He wants to make his mind up—once and for all.
He wants to make his mind up who he is going with.

5 BILLY. I haven't seen Liz for three months.

6 ALICE. Well, who were you with then? Down at Foley
Bottoms? Last night?

7 BILLY. Rita.

8 GEOFFREY. Who the bloody hell's Rita?

9 FLORENCE. She wants to see that he makes his mind up.

10 ALICE. I shall tell Barbara this afternoon—I shall tell her,
make no mistake about that.

11 GEOFFREY. He's never satisfied with what he has got—that's
his bloody trouble. He never has been. It's ever since he
left school. It's ever since he took that job—clerking.
Clerking for that undertaker—what kind of a bloody
job's that?

12 BILLY. Perhaps I might not be doing it much longer.

13 GEOFFREY. You what?

14 ALICE. What do you mean?

15 BILLY. I've been offered a job in London.

16 GEOFFREY [*turning away in disgust*]. Don't talk bloody wet.

17 ALICE. How do you mean? A job in London? What job in
London?

18 BILLY [*taking a crumpled envelope from his raincoat pocket*]. What I say,
I've been offered a job in London. Script-writing.

19 GEOFFREY. Bloody script-writing.

1   ALICE. What script-writing?

2   GEOFFREY. Script-writing! He can't write his bloody name so you can read it. Who'd set him on?

3   BILLY [*proudly*]. Danny Boon.

4   ALICE. Danny who?

5   BILLY [*going into a slow, exasperated explanation*]. I told you before. Boon. Danny Boon. I told you. He was on at the Empire the week before last. When he was there I told you. I went to see him. I went to his dressing-room. I took him some of my scripts. Well, he's read them. He's read them and he likes them. And he's sent me this letter. He's offered me a job in London. Script-writing. Danny Boon. The comedian. He's been on television.

6   FLORENCE [*addressing the television*]. It's always boxing; boxing and horse shows.

7   ALICE [*ignoring her*]. Danny Boon? I don't remember ever seeing him.

8   GEOFFREY. No, and neither does anybody else. It's another of his tales. Danny Boon! He's made him up.

9   ALICE. What kind of a job?

10 BILLY. I've told you. Script-writing.

11 GEOFFREY. It's like all these other tales he comes home with. He can't say two words to anybody without it's a bloody lie. And what's he been telling that woman in the fish shop about me having my leg off? Do I look as though I've had my leg off?

12 BILLY. It wasn't you. It was Barbara's uncle. She gets everything wrong—that woman in the fish shop.

13 ALICE. You'll have to stop all this making things up, Billy. There's no sense in it at your age. We never know where we are with you. I mean, you're too old for things like that now.

14 BILLY [*displaying the letter*]. Look—all right then. I've got the letter—here. He wants me to go down to see him. In

8

London. To fix things up. I'm going to ring up this morning and give them my notice.

2 ALICE. You can't do things like that, Billy. You can't just go dashing off to London on spec.

3 GEOFFREY [*disparagingly*]. He's not going to no bloody London. It's them that'll be ringing him up, more like. You'll get the sack—I'll tell you what you'll get. What time are you supposed to be going in there this morning, anyroad?

4 BILLY. I'm not. It's my Saturday off this week.

5 GEOFFREY. You said that last bloody week. That's three bloody weeks in a row.

6 BILLY. I got mixed up.

7 GEOFFREY. I've no patience with you. [*He places the invoices in his pocket and rises from his chair.*] Anyway, I've got some work to do if you haven't.

8 ALICE. Are you going in towards town, Geoffrey?

9 GEOFFREY. I'm going in that direction.

10 ALICE. You can drop me off. I'm going down as far as the shops.

11 GEOFFREY. I can if you're not going to be all bloody day getting ready. I'm late now.

12 ALICE [*crossing towards the hall*]. I'm ready now. I've only to slip my coat on.

ALICE *goes out into the hall and puts on a coat which is hanging on the rack.* GEOFFREY *turns to* BILLY.

13 GEOFFREY. And you can get your mucky self washed—and get bloody dressed. And keep your bloody hands off my razor else you'll know about it.

14 FLORENCE [*raising her voice*]. Is she going past Driver's? 'Cause there's that pork pie to pick up for this afternoon's tea.

ALICE *re-enters the living-room.*

1   ALICE. I'm ready. I'll call in for that pie. [*To* BILLY.] Your breakfast's on the kitchen table. It'll be clap-cold by now.

2   GEOFFREY [*crossing towards the door. He turns for a final sally at* BILLY]. And you can wash them pots up when you've finished. Don't leave it all for your mother.

3   ALICE. I shan't be above an hour, Mother.

    ALICE *and* GEOFFREY *go out through the hall and into the garden.* BILLY *goes into the kitchen.*

4   FLORENCE. I shouldn't be left on my own. She's not said anything now about the insurance man. I don't know what to give him if he comes.

    ALICE *and* GEOFFREY *are moving down the garden.*

5   GEOFFREY. I'm only going as far as the lane, you know, I don't know why you can't get the bloody bus.

    ALICE *and* GEOFFREY *exeunt.* BILLY *re-enters from the kitchen. He is carrying a cup and a teapot.*

6   BILLY. I can't eat that egg. It's stone cold.

7   FLORENCE. There's too much waste in this house. It's all goodness just thrown down the sink. We had it to eat. When I was his age we couldn't leave nothing. If we didn't eat it then it was put out the next meal. When we had eggs, that was. We were lucky to get them. You had to make do with what there was. Bread and dripping.

8   BILLY [*sitting down he pours himself a cup of tea*]. Do you want a cup of tea?

9   FLORENCE. And if you weren't down at six o'clock of a morning you didn't get that.

10 BILLY [*he drinks and grimaces*]. They don't drink tea in London at this time of a morning. It's all coffee. That's what I'll be doing this time next week.

1 FLORENCE. Sundays was just the same. No lying-in then.

   BILLY *and his grandmother are now in their own separate dream-worlds.*

2 BILLY. Sitting in a coffee-bar. Espresso. With a girl. Art student. Duffle-coat and dirty toe-nails. I discovered her the night before. Contemplating suicide.

3 FLORENCE. If you had a job in them days you had to stick to it. You couldn't get another.

4 BILLY [*addressing his imaginary companion*]. Nothing is as bad as it seems, my dear. Less than a week ago my father felt the same as you. Suicidal. He came round after the operation and looked down where his legs should have been. Nothing.

5 FLORENCE. We couldn't go traipsing off to London or anywhere else. If we got as far as Scarborough we were lucky.

6 BILLY. Just an empty space in the bed. Well, he'll never be World Champion now. A broken man on two tin legs.

   BILLY *slowly levers himself out of his chair and limps slowly and painfully around the room leaning heavily against the furniture.*

7 FLORENCE [*addressing* BILLY *in the third person*]. He's not right in the head.

   BILLY *realizes he is being watched and comes out of his fantasy.*

   I wouldn't care, but it makes me poorly watching him.

8 BILLY [*rubbing his leg and by way of explanation*]. Cramp.

9 FLORENCE. He wants to get his-self dressed.

   ARTHUR CRABTREE *enters the garden and approaches the front door. He is about the same age as* BILLY. *He is wearing flannels, a sports coat and a loud checked shirt. He pushes the door-bell which rings out in two tones in the hall.*

   [*As* BILLY *crosses to answer the bell.*] He shouldn't be going to the door dressed like that.

   BILLY *opens the door and, together with* ARTHUR, *goes into a routine—their usual way of greeting each other.* ARTHUR *holds up an imaginary lantern and peers into an imaginary darkness.*

1 ARTHUR [*in a thick north-country accent*]. There's trouble up at the mill.

2 BILLY [*also in a thick north-country accent*]. What's afoot, Ned Leather? Is Willy Arkwright smashing up my looms again?

3 ARTHUR. It's the men! They'll not stand for that lad of yours down from Oxford and Cambridge.

4 BILLY. They'll stand for him and lump it. There's allus been an Oldroyd at Oldroyd's mill and there allus will be.

5 ARTHUR. Nay, Josiah! He's upsetting them with his fancy college ways and they'll have none of it. They're on the march! They're coming up the drive!

6 BILLY. Into the house, Ned, and bar the door! We've got to remember our Sal's condition.

They enter together and march into the living-room where they both dissolve into laughter.

7 FLORENCE. Carrying on and making a commotion. It's worse than Bedlam. Carrying on and all that noise. They want to make less noise, the pair of them.

8 ARTHUR. Good morning, Mrs. Boothroyd.

9 FLORENCE. He wants to make less noise and get his-self dressed.

10 BILLY. Do you want a cup of tea, Arthur? I'm just having my breakfast.

11 ARTHUR. You rotten idle crow! Some of us have done a day's work already, you lazy get.

12 BILLY. Why aren't you at work now?

13 ARTHUR. Why aren't you at rotten work, that's why I'm not at work. Come to see where you are. They're going bonkers at the office. You never turned in last Saturday either.

14 BILLY. Isn't it my Saturday off this week?

15 ARTHUR. You know rotten well it isn't.

1   FLORENCE [getting up from the couch]. They're all idle. They're all
    the same. They make me badly.

    FLORENCE crosses the room and disappears up the stairs into the
    bedroom.

2   BILLY. I could say I forgot and thought it was.

3   ARTHUR. You can hellers like. You said that last week.

4   BILLY. Tell them my grandad's had his leg off.

5   ARTHUR. You haven't got a rotten grandad. Anyroad, I can't
    tell them anything. I'm not supposed to have seen you.
    I've come up in my break. I'm supposed to be having
    my coffee. I'm not telling them anything. I'm having
    enough bother as it is with our old lady. What with you
    and your lousy stories. Telling everybody she was in
    the family way. She's heard about it. She says she's
    going to come up here and see your father.

6   BILLY. Cripes, she can't do that! It was only last night I told
    him she'd just had a miscarriage. She's not supposed to
    be up yet.

7   ARTHUR. What the hell did you tell him that for?

8   BILLY. I hadn't any choice. My mother was going to send a
    present round for the baby.

9   ARTHUR. The trouble with you, cocker, is you're just a
    rotten pathological liar. Anyway, you've done it this
    time. You've dropped yourself right in with not
    coming in this morning.

10 BILLY. I can get out of that. I'll think of some excuse.

11 ARTHUR. There's more to it than that, matey. Shadrack's
    been going through your postage book.

12 BILLY. When?

13 ARTHUR. This morning, when do you think? There's nearly
    three rotten quid short. All there is in the book is one
    stinking lousy rotten threepenny stamp and he says he
    gave you two pound ten stamp money on Wednesday.

14 BILLY. Fizzing hell! Has he been through the petty cash as
    well?

1 ARTHUR. Not when I left. No. Why, have you been fiddling that as well?

2 BILLY. No, no . . . I haven't filled the book up, though.

3 ARTHUR. And he was going on about some calendars—I don't know what he meant.

4 BILLY [*crossing to the sideboard*]. I do.

> BILLY *takes a small key from his raincoat pocket and opens the right-hand cupboard. As he does so a pile of large envelopes fall out on to the carpet followed by a few odds and ends.*

There you are, Tosh, two hundred and sixty of the bastards.

5 ARTHUR. What?

6 BILLY. Maring calendars.

7 ARTHUR [*crosses and picks up an envelope from the floor*]. What do you want with two rotten hundred and sixty calendars? [*He reads the address on the front of the envelope.*] 'The Mother Superior, The Convent of the Sacred Heart!'

> *He tears open the envelope and takes out a large, wall calendar illustrated with a colourful painting of a kitten and a dog. He reads the inscription.*

'Shadrack and Duxbury, Funeral Furnishers.' These are the firm's! 'Taste, Tact and Economy.' You skiving nit! You should have posted these last Christmas.

8 BILLY. Yes.

9 ARTHUR. Well, what are they doing in your sideboard cupboard?

10 BILLY. I never had enough stamps in the postage book.

11 ARTHUR. You think that postage money's part of your bloody wages, don't you?

> *He bends down and sorts through the pile of papers on the floor.*

Why do you keep them in there?

12 BILLY. It's where I keep all my private things.

1 ARTHUR [*picking up a small package*]. Private things! A naffing crêpe bandage!

He throws down the package and picks up a piece of blue note-paper.

What's this then?

2 BILLY [*making a grab for the letter*]. Gerroff, man! Give us that here! That's personal!

3 ARTHUR [*evading* BILLY'S *hand*]. What the hell are you writing to Godfrey Winn for?

4 BILLY. It's not me. It's my mother.

5 ARTHUR [*reading the letter*]. 'Dear Sir, Just a few lines to let you know how much I enjoy "Housewives' Choice" every day, I always listen no matter what I am doing, could you play "Just a Song at Twilight" for me.' That's a turn-up for the top-ten! She isn't half with it, your old lady! [*Reading.*] 'I don't suppose you get time to play everyone that writes to you, but this is my favourite song. You see my husband often used to sing it when we were a bit younger than we are now. I will quite understand if you cannot play. Your respectfully Mrs. A. Fisher.' So why didn't you post this then?

6 BILLY. I couldn't be bothered. [*He makes a further attempt to grab the letter.*] Give us it here!

7 ARTHUR [*holding him off*]. 'P.S. My son also writes songs, but I suppose there is not much chance for him as he has not had the training. We are just ordinary folk.'

8 BILLY [*snatches the letter and tosses it into the cupboard*]. I'm not ordinary folk even if she is. [*He crams the envelopes containing the calendars back into the cupboard.*] I keep trying to get rid of them. It was bad enough getting them out of the office.

9 ARTHUR. How long have they been here?

10 BILLY. Not long. I used to keep them in that coffin in the basement at work. You can't get rid of the fizzing things! It's like a bloody nightmare. They won't burn.

I've tried tearing them up and pushing them down the lavatory—all they do is float.

2 ARTHUR. Makes no difference what you do with them. Duxbury's on to you. He knows about them.

3 BILLY [*stuffing the last of the calendars into the cupboard he locks the door*]. Oh well . . . so what. He knows what he can do with his calendars. I don't give a monkey's. I'm leaving. I've got another job.

4 ARTHUR. Leaving?

5 BILLY. I'm going to ring him up this morning and give him my notice.

6 ARTHUR. Yes, and we've heard that one before.

7 BILLY. No, straight up. I'm going to London.

8 ARTHUR. What as—road-sweeper?

9 BILLY [*grandiloquently*]. Ay road sweepah on the road—to fame! [*He returns to his normal voice.*] I've got that job with Danny Boon.

10 ARTHUR. You haven't!

11 BILLY. Yes—script-writer. Start next week.

12 ARTHUR. You jammy burk! Have you though, honest?

13 BILLY. Yeh—course I have. It's all fixed up. He sent me a letter. Asking me to work for him.

14 ARTHUR. What's he paying you?

15 BILLY. A cowing sight more than I get from Shadrack and flaming Duxbury's.

16 ARTHUR. What? Counting the postage?

17 BILLY. What's it to you? This is it for me, boy! Success! 'Saturday Night Spectacular!' 'Sunday Night at the Palladium!' Script by!

18 ARTHUR. Ta-ra-ra-raaa!

19 BILLY. Billy Fisher! Directed by!

20 ARTHUR. Ta-ra-ra-raaa!

21 BILLY. William Fisher! Produced by!

1 ARTHUR. Ta-ra-ra-raaa!

2 BILLY. William S. Fisher!

3 ARTHUR. Ta-ra-ra-raaa!

4 BILLY. A W. S. Fisher Presentation! 'Mr. Fisher, on behalf of the British Television Industry, serving the needs of twenty million viewers, it gives me great pleasure to present you with this award, this evening, in recognition of the fact that you have been voted Television Script-writer of the Year—for the seventh year running.'

5 ARTHUR [*picking up a vase from the sideboard he places it in* BILLY'S *hands*]. Big-head.

6 BILLY [*returning the vase to the sideboard*]. Rot off. You wait and see.

7 ARTHUR [*taking a small bottle of tablets from his trouser pocket*]. So you won't be needing these now, then, will you?

8 BILLY. What's them?

9 ARTHUR. Passion pills. What I said I'd get for you.

10 BILLY [*taking the bottle incredulously*]. Let's have a look, mate. [*He opens the bottle and is about to swallow one of the tablets.*] What do they taste like?

11 ARTHUR. Here, go steady on, man! They'll give you the screaming ab-dabs.

12 BILLY [*returning the tablet to the bottle*]. How did you get hold of them?

13 ARTHUR. From a mate of mine who got demobbed. He brought them back from Singapore.

14 BILLY. I'll bet they're bloody aspirins.

15 ARTHUR. Do you want to bet? You want to ask this bloke, tosher.

16 BILLY. How many do you give them?

17 ARTHUR. Just one. Two two-and-nines at the Regal, a bag of chips and one of these and you're away. Who's it for anyway?

18 BILLY. Barbara . . . Bloody hell!

1   ARTHUR. What's up?

2   BILLY. She's supposed to be coming round this morning.

3   ARTHUR. I thought it was this afternoon? For her tea?

4   BILLY [*placing the bottle of tablets on the sideboard*]. No, I've got to see her first. Our old man'll go bald if he sees her before I've had a word with her. She thinks he's in the Merchant Navy.

5   ARTHUR. You what?

6   BILLY [*crossing hurriedly towards the hall*]. On petrol tankers. [*He indicates the tea-things.*] Shift them into the kitchen for me. Shan't be a tick.

> BILLY *runs up the stairs in the hall and into his bedroom.* ARTHUR *picks up the teapot and goes into the kitchen.* ARTHUR *re-enters and crosses to the sideboard where he picks up the bottle of tablets.* BILLY *appears at the top of the stairs with his clothes in his hands.* BILLY *moves down the stairs and enters the living-room.* ARTHUR *replaces the tablets on the sideboard.*

7   ARTHUR. What time's she supposed to be coming?

8   BILLY [*dressing hastily*]. Quarter of an hour since. Where's them passion pills?

9   ARTHUR. On the sideboard. You're not going to slip her one this morning are you?

10   BILLY. Why not? I'm pressed for time, man. I'm going out with Rita tonight.

11   ARTHUR. Well, what about your grandmother?

12   BILLY. Oh, she's spark out till dinner-time.

13   ARTHUR. I've lost track of your rotten sex life. Which one are you supposed to be engaged to, anyway?

14   BILLY. That's what they call an academic question.

15   ARTHUR. Well, you can't be engaged to both of them at once, for God's sake.

16   BILLY. Do you want to bet?

17   ARTHUR. Crikey! Well, which of them's got the naffing engagement ring?

1 BILLY. Well, that's the trouble. That's partly the reason why Barbara's coming round this morning—if she did but know it. She's got it. I've got to get it off her. For Rita.

2 ARTHUR. What for?

3 BILLY. Ah, well . . . You see, she had it first—Rita. Only I got it from her to give to Barbara. Now she wants it back. I told her it was at the jeweller's—getting the stone fixed. There'll be hell to pay if she doesn't get it.

4 ARTHUR. The sooner you get to London the better.

5 BILLY [*tucking his shirt in his trousers and slipping on his jacket*]. Are you sure them passion pills'll work on Barbara? She's dead from the neck down.

6 ARTHUR. You haven't tried.

7 BILLY. Tried! Who hasn't tried! If you want to try you're welcome. All she does is sit and eat stinking oranges.

8 ARTHUR. What I can't work out is why you got engaged to her in the first place. What's wrong with Liz?

9 BILLY. Don't talk to me about Liz. I've not seen her for months. She's tooled off to Bradford or somewhere.

10 ARTHUR. Well, she's tooled back again then. I saw her this morning.

11 BILLY. What? Liz?

12 ARTHUR. Yeh—scruffy Lizzie. I bumped into her in Sheepgate. Mucky as ever. It's about time somebody bought her a new skirt.

BARBARA approches the house. She is about nineteen years old, a large well-built girl in a tweed suit and flat-heeled shoes. She is carrying a large handbag.

13 BILLY. Did she say anything about me?

14 ARTHUR. I didn't stop. Just said 'Hello'. I wouldn't be seen stood standing talking to that scruffy-looking bird.

BARBARA rings the bell.

1   BILLY. That's Barbara! Where's them passion pills!

BILLY *crosses and taking the bottle from the sideboard he places it in his breast pocket.* ARTHUR *crosses towards the door.*

2   ARTHUR. I'll have to get going, anyway. I'll get shot when I get back to work. I've been gone nearly half an hour now.

3   BILLY [*crossing towards the door*]. Hang on a couple of minutes, man. Don't make it look too obvious! If she sees you going out and leaving her with me she'll be out of that door like a whippet.

4   ARTHUR. I'm late now!

5   BILLY. You can chat her up for a minute.

BILLY *crosses into the hall and opens the door to admit* BARBARA.

Hallo, darling!

6   BARBARA [*who uses endearments coldly and flatly*]. Hallo, pet.

7   BILLY [*leading the way*]. Come through into the lounge.

8   BARBARA [*following* BILLY *into the living-room*]. Hallo, Arthur.

ARTHUR *winks at her.* BARBARA *looks round the room.*

What a nice room! [*She crosses to examine the cocktail cabinet.*] What a beautiful cocktail cabinet!

9   BILLY. I made it.

ARTHUR *reacts to this statement.*

10   BARBARA. How clever of you, sweet. I didn't know you could do woodwork.

11   BILLY. Oh yes, I made all the furniture. [*A pause and then, wildly.*] And the garage.

BARBARA *looks around the room doubtfully.*

12   ARTHUR [*coughs*]. It's time I was making a move, mate.

13   BARBARA. You're not going because of me, Arthur?

14   ARTHUR. No, I'm supposed to be at work. [*To* BILLY.] So long, Tosh!

1   BILLY. So long.

2   BARBARA. Bye! . . . Isn't your sister in, Billy?

3   ARTHUR [*stops short on his way to the door and turns*]. What bloody
    sister?

> BILLY, *unnoticed by* BARBARA, *gesticulates to* ARTHUR *to leave.*
> ARTHUR *does so—hastily.*

4   BILLY. Barbara, I'm glad you asked me that question. About
    my sister.

5   BARBARA. What is it?

6   BILLY. Sit down, darling. [BARBARA *sits on the couch.*] Darling, are
    you still coming to tea this afternoon?

7   BARBARA. Of course.

8   BILLY. Because there are some things I want to tell you.

9   BARBARA. What things, Billy?

10 BILLY. You know what you said the other night—about
    loving me? Even if I were a criminal.

11 BARBARA. Well?

12 BILLY. You said you'd still love me even if I'd murdered your
    mother.

13 BARBARA [*suspiciously*]. Well?

14 BILLY. I wonder if you'll still love me when you hear what
    I've got to say. You see—well, you know that I've got a
    fairly vivid imagination, don't you?

15 BARBARA. Well, you have to have if you're going to be a
    script-writer, don't you?

16 BILLY. Well, being a script-writer, I'm perhaps—at times—a
    bit inclined to let my imagination run away with me.
    As you know. [BARBARA *is even more aloof than usual.*] You
    see, the thing is, if we're going to have our life together
    —and that cottage—and little Billy and little Barbara
    and the lily pond and all that . . . Well, there's some
    things we've got to get cleared up.

17 BARBARA. What things?

1   BILLY. Some of the things I'm afraid I've been telling you.

2   BARBARA. Do you mean you've been telling me lies?

3   BILLY. Well, not lies exactly . . . But I suppose I've been, well, exaggerating some things. Being a script-writer . . . For instance, there's that business about my father. Him being a sea captain. On a petrol tanker.

4   BARBARA. You mean he's not on a petrol tanker?

5   BILLY. He's not even in the navy.

6   BARBARA. Well, what is he?

7   BILLY. He's in the removal business.

8   BARBARA. And what about him being a prisoner-of-war? And that tunnel? And the medal? Don't say that was all lies?

9   BILLY. Yes. [BARBARA *turns away abruptly.*] Are you cross?

10 BARBARA. No—not cross. Just disappointed. It sounds as though you were ashamed of your father.

11 BILLY. I'm not ashamed. I'm not—I'm not!

12 BARBARA. Otherwise why say he was a prisoner-of-war? What was he?

13 BILLY. A conscientious ob . . . [*He checks himself.*] He wasn't anything. He wasn't fit. He has trouble with his knee.

14 BARBARA. The knee he's supposed to have been shot in, I suppose.

15 BILLY. Yes. Another thing, we haven't got a budgie, or a cat. And I didn't make the furniture . . . Not all of it, any-way.

16 BARBARA. How many other lies have you been telling me?

17 BILLY. My sister.

18 BARBARA. Don't tell me you haven't got a sister.

19 BILLY. I did have. But she's dead. If you're still coming for your tea this afternoon they never talk about her.

BARBARA *remains silent, her head still turned away.*

You remind me of her . . . If you're not coming, I'll

understand . . . I'm just not good enough for you, Barbara . . . If you want to give me the engagement ring back—I'll understand.

2 BARBARA [*turning towards him*]. Don't be cross with yourself, Billy. I forgive you.

3 BILLY [*moving to kiss her*]. Darling. . . .

4 BARBARA [*moving away*]. But promise me one thing.

5 BILLY. That I'll never lie to you again? [BARBARA *nods.*] I'll never lie to you again. Never, I promise . . . Darling, there is one thing. I have got a grannie.

6 BARBARA. I believe you.

7 BILLY. Only she's not blind. She's not very well, though. She's upstairs. Sleeping. She might have to have her leg off.

8 BARBARA [*kissing him*]. Poor darling.

9 BILLY [*moving quickly towards the cocktail cabinet*]. Would you like a drink?

10 BARBARA. Not now, pet.

11 BILLY [*opening the cabinet*]. Port. To celebrate.

12 BARBARA. All right. Well, just a tiny one.

13 BILLY. I'm turning over a new leaf.

Unnoticed to BARBARA *he pours the drink and taking a tablet from the 'passion pill' bottle, places it in her glass. He crosses with the glasses and sits beside her on the couch.*

That's yours darling.

14 BARBARA [*sitting on the edge of the couch she sips the port*]. Let's talk about something nice.

15 BILLY. Let's talk about our cottage.

16 BARBARA. Oh, I've seen the most marvellous material to make curtains for the living-room. Honestly, you'll love it. It's a sort of turquoise with lovely little squiggles like wine-glasses.

17 BILLY. Will it go with the yellow carpet?

1 BARBARA. No, but it will go with the grey rugs.

2 BILLY [*taking her in his arms*]. I love you, darling.

3 BARBARA [*moving away*]. I love you.

4 BILLY. Do you? Really and truly?

5 BARBARA. Of course I do.

6 BILLY. Are you looking forward to getting married?

> BARBARA *takes an orange from her handbag and peels it and eats
> it during the following dialogue.*

7 BARBARA. I think about it every minute of the day.

8 BILLY. Darling . . . [*He again attempts unsuccessfully to kiss her.*] Don't
ever fall in love with anybody else.

9 BARBARA. Let's talk about our cottage.

10 BILLY [*simulating a dreamy voice*]. What about our cottage?

11 BARBARA. About the garden..Tell me about the garden.

12 BILLY. We'll have a lovely garden. We'll have roses in it and
daffodils and a lovely lawn with a swing for little Billy
and little Barbara to play on. And we'll have our meals·
down by the lily pond in summer.

13 BARBARA. Do you think a lily pond is safe? What if the
kiddies wandered too near and fell in?

14 BILLY. We'll build a wall round it. No—no, we won't. We
won't have a pond at all. We'll have an old well. An old
brick well where we draw the water. We'll make it our
wishing well. Do you know what I'll wish?

15 BARBARA [*shaking her head*]. No.

16 BILLY. Tell me what you'll wish first.

17 BARBARA. Oh, I'll wish that we'll always be happy. And
always love each other. What will you wish?

18 BILLY. Better not tell you.

19 BARBARA. Why not, pet?

20 BILLY. You might be cross.

21 BARBARA. Why would I be cross?

1 BILLY. Oh, I don't know . . . You might think me too . . .
   well, forward. [*He glances at her face but can see no reaction.*]
   Barbara. . . .? Do you think it's wrong for people to
   have—you know, feelings?

2 BARBARA. Not if they're genuinely in love with each other.

3 BILLY. Like we are.

4 BARBARA [*uncertainly*]. Yes.

5 BILLY. Would you think it wrong of me to have—feelings?

6 BARBARA [*briskly and firmly*]. I think we ought to be married
   first.

7 BILLY [*placing his hand on* BARBARA'S *knee*]. Darling. . . .

8 BARBARA. Are you feeling all right?

9 BILLY. Of course, darling. Why?

10 BARBARA. Look where your hand is.

11 BILLY. Darling, don't you want me to touch you?

12 BARBARA [*shrugging*]. It seems . . . indecent, somehow.

13 BILLY. Are you feeling all right?

14 BARBARA. Yes, of course.

15 BILLY. How do you feel?

16 BARBARA. Contented.

17 BILLY. You don't feel . . . you know—restless?

18 BARBARA. No.

19 BILLY. Finish your drink.

20 BARBARA. In a minute. [*She opens her handbag and offers it towards
   him.*] Have an orange.

   BILLY *snatching the bag from her he throws it down and oranges spill
   out across the floor.*

21 BILLY. You and your bloody oranges!

22 BARBARA [*remonstratively*]. Billy! . . . Darling!

23 BILLY [*placing his head on her shoulder*]. I'm sorry, darling. I've had
   a terrible morning.

1 BARBARA. Why? What's happened?

2 BILLY. Oh, nothing. The usual. Family and things. Just that I've got a headache.

3 BARBARA. I'm sorry, pet. You know, you ought to see a doctor.

4 BILLY. I've seen doctors—specialists—I've seen them all. All they could give me was a crêpe bandage. [BARBARA, *unimpressed, licks her fingers.*] You know, my darling, I think you have feelings, too. Deep down.

5 BARBARA [*examining her hands distastefully*]. Oooh, sticky paws!

6 BILLY. Wipe them on the cushion. [*He rises as a thought strikes him.*] You can go upstairs if you want. Use our bathroom.

7 BARBARA. Thank you.

> BARBARA, *picking up her handbag, crosses into the hall and goes upstairs.* BILLY *picks up her glass and crosses to the cocktail cabinet, where he pours out two more drinks. Taking the 'passion pills' from his pocket, he adds two pills to* BARBARA'S *glass and then, on impulse, he adds the entire contents of the bottle into her glass. He is standing admiring the glass and its contents as the telephone rings in the hall. He places the glass on the table and crosses into the hall where he picks up the phone.*

8 BILLY. The Fisher residence? Can I help you? [*His manner changes.*] Oh, hullo, Mr. Duxbury. No, well, I'm sorry but I've had an accident. I was just leaving for work and I spilt this hot water down my arm. I had to get it bandaged . . . Oh, well, I think there's a very simple explanation for that, Mr. Duxbury. You see, there's a lot of those figures that haven't been carried forward . . . I use my own individual system . . . No. No, not me, Mr. Duxbury. Well, I'm sure you'll find that there's a very simple explanation . . . What? Monday morning? Yes, of course I'll be there. Prompt. Thank you, Mr. Duxbury. Thank you for ringing. Good-bye, then . . . [BILLY *puts down the telephone for a moment and is lost in depression.*

He brightens as, in his imagination, he addresses his employer.]
Well, look Duxbury—we're not going to argue over
trivialities. As soon as I've finalized my arrangements
with Mr. Boon I'll get in touch with you. [*He picks up the
telephone.*] Hello, Duxbury? . . . I'm afraid the answer is
'no'. I fully agree that a partnership sounds very
attractive—but frankly my interests lie in other direc-
tions. I'm quite willing to invest in your business, but
I just have not the time to take over the administrative
side . . . Oh, I agree that you have a sound proposition
there . . . Granted! I take your point, Mr. Duxbury.
What's that little saying of yours? 'You've got to come
down to earth.' It's not a question of coming down to
earth, old man. Some of us belong in the stars. The best
of luck, Mr. Duxbury, and keep writing . . . [BILLY *breaks
off as* BARBARA *approaches down the stairs and, for her benefit, he
goes off into another fantasy as she passes him and enters the living-
room.*] Well, doctor, if the leg's got to come off—it's got
to come off . . . [BILLY *replaces the telephone and looks specu-
latively at the living-room door.*] It's not a question of coming
down to earth, Mr. Duxbury. [*He pauses.*] Some of us,
Mr. Duxbury, belong in the stars.

BILLY, *who has now regained his self-confidence, enters the living-
room and crosses towards* BARBARA *with her glass of port.*

THE CURTAIN FALLS

✷ ✷ ✷
Act 2

It is late afernoon the same day and just after tea-time in the FISHER household.
ALICE is moving in and out of the kitchen clearing the tea-things from the living-
room table. The best tea-service has been brought out for BARBARA's benefit,
although FLORENCE has insisted upon having her usual pint-pot. A strange
silence has fallen upon the living-room caused partly by BARBARA's disclosure
that she has recently become engaged to BILLY—and partly by FLORENCE's
insistence on taking her time over her tea. FLORENCE, in fact, is the only one
remaining at the table. GEOFFREY has moved away to a chair and BARBARA is
seated on the couch. BILLY is in the hall engaged in a phone conversation and has
closed the door to the living-room.

1 BILLY. . . . Rita, will you listen for a minute! . . . No, listen to
    what I'm telling you! The ring's still at the jeweller's!
    Of course it's all right . . . Well, what's the sense in
    coming round here now! It isn't here—I've just told
    you, it's at the jeweller's . . . Rita! . . . [*He puts down*
    the phone.] Oh blimey! . . . [*He takes up the phone and dials a*
    number.]

2 BARBARA [*in an attempt to break the silence*]. Of course, we haven't
    fixed the date or anything. [*There is a pause.*] We won't be
    thinking of getting married for quite a while yet.

3 GEOFFREY [*a slight pause*]. Well, what you going to live on? The
    pair of you? He'll never have a bloody penny.

4 FLORENCE. And there was none of this hire purchase in them
    days. What you couldn't pay for you didn't have. I don't
    agree with it. He didn't either. It's only muck and
    rubbish when it's there.

    ALICE returns from the kitchen and fills a tray with used tea-things.
    She picks up FLORENCE's pint-pot.

    I haven't finished with that yet. [*ALICE replaces the pot.*]

    BILLY puts down the phone in exasperation. He picks it up and dials
    another number. ALICE returns to the kitchen with the tray.

1   BARBARA. We had thought of a cottage in Devon.

2   GEOFFREY. Bloody Devon! He'll never get past the end of our street.

3   FLORENCE. She needn't have opened that tin of salmon—it's not been touched hardly.

4   BARBARA. I don't believe in long engagements—but I don't mind waiting.

5   GEOFFREY. You'll wait till bloody Domesday if you wait for that sackless article. He's not had a shave yet.

6   ALICE [*putting her head round the kitchen door*]. Come on, Mother! It's only you we're waiting for.

7   FLORENCE [*mumbling to herself*]. She knows I haven't got to be rushed. I don't know what she does it for. . . .

An awkward silence falls upon the living-room. BILLY *speaks into the telephone.*

8   BILLY. Arthur? . . . Look, you've got to do something for me. Stop Rita coming round here . . . Well, go round to their house! She's after the ring and Barbara's still got it . . . No, did she heckerslike! I told you they were aspirins. Don't stand there yattering, get your skates on!

He slams down the receiver.

9   FLORENCE [*who has been mumbling quietly to herself throughout the above now raises her voice to address the sideboard*]. It's every tea-time alike. Rush, rush, rush. They've got no consideration. She knows I'm not well.

10 BARBARA [*politely*]. Billy was saying you'd not been well.

11 GEOFFREY. Take no notice of what he says—he'll have you as bloody daft as his-self. [BILLY *opens the door and enters the living-room.*] You'll stand talking on that phone till you look like a bloody telephone. Who was it, then?

12 BILLY. Only Arthur.

13 GEOFFREY. What's he bloody want?

14 BILLY. Oh—nothing.

1   GEOFFREY. He takes his time asking for it.

2   ALICE [*enters from the kitchen*]. How's his mother?

3   BILLY [*crossing to the fireplace*]. All right—considering.

4   BARBARA. Arthur's mother? Has she been ill?

5   GEOFFREY. That's the bloody tale he's come home with.

6   BILLY [*shuffling awkwardly in front of the fire*]. She's been off-colour, but she's all right.

7   GEOFFREY. By, if I don't knock some sense into you! Stand up straight and get your hands out of your pockets! You want to get married, you do!

8   FLORENCE. She wants to sew them up. With a needle and cotton. She should sew them up.

9   GEOFFREY. You'll have to brighten your ideas up, then!

10 FLORENCE. A needle and a bit of black cotton. That'd stop him. Then he couldn't put them in his pockets.

11 ALICE. Mother, haven't you finished that tea yet! Why don't you finish it by the fire. I've got to get cleared up.

12 FLORENCE [*rising and crossing slowly to sit by the fire*]. I can't be up and down—up and down—every five minutes. She knows it doesn't do me any good. And that fire's too hot. He banks it up till it's like a furnace in here. I can't be putting up with it.

13 ALICE [*clearing the remains off the table*]. Well, it's all very well, Mother, I like to get things done. Then it's finished with.

14 BARBARA. Can I be giving you a hand, Mrs. Fisher?

15 ALICE. It's all right, Barbara. I don't know why our Billy doesn't wash up once in a while.

16 GEOFFREY. He can't wash his bloody self, never mind the pots.

17 BARBARA [*rising and crossing towards the kitchen*]. I don't mind.

BARBARA *and* ALICE *go off into the kitchen.* BILLY *crosses to sit on the couch and* GEOFFREY *rises. There is an embarrassed silence. There is a first attempt at contact between* BILLY *and his father.*

1 GEOFFREY. She doesn't have much to say for herself . . . Where do you say she works, then?

2 BILLY. Turnbull and Mason's.

3 GEOFFREY. Who?

4 BILLY. Solicitors. Up Sheepgate.

5 GEOFFREY. Oh aye?

6 BILLY. Shorthand-typist.

7 GEOFFREY. She likes her food, doesn't she? She'll take some keeping. By bloody hell! She had her share of that pork pie, didn't she?

8 BILLY. She lives up Cragside. On that new estate.

9 GEOFFREY. She'll need to live up Cragside the way she eats. She can shift them tinned oranges when she starts, can't she? Mind you, she needs it. She's a big lass, isn't she? Big-boned.

10 BILLY. Yes.

11 GEOFFREY [after a pause]. You're reckoning on getting married then?

12 BILLY. Thinking about it.

13 GEOFFREY. You've got your bloody self engaged, anyroad.

14 BILLY. Yes.

15 GEOFFREY. So she was saying. You never told us.

16 BILLY. No. I was meaning to.

17 GEOFFREY. That was a bit of a daft trick to do, wasn't it?

18 BILLY. Oh, I don't know.

19 GEOFFREY. I mean, at your age like. You're only young yet. You're not old enough to start thinking about getting married.

20 BILLY. There's no hurry.

21 GEOFFREY. No. But you'll have to put your mind to it some time.

22 BILLY. Yes.

1 GEOFFREY. I mean, you can't go carrying-on the way you've
      been carrying-on—now, you know. Messing about with
      different lasses.

2 BILLY. No—I know. I realize that.

3 GEOFFREY. You've not only yourself to consider. I don't see
      why you couldn't have waited a bit. I don't see why you
      couldn't have told us—your mother and me.

4 BILLY. I've said—I was meaning to.

5 GEOFFREY. She's not—you haven't got her into trouble—
      mean, there's nothing like that about it, is there?

6 BILLY. No . . . No—'course not.

   BILLY *looks across at his father and we feel, for a moment, that they
   are about to make some point of contact.*

7 GEOFFREY. Well, that's something, anyroad. I suppose she's
      all right. Just with you not saying anything, that's all.

8 BILLY. Yes.

9 GEOFFREY. Only you'll have to start thinking about getting
      married. Saving up and that.

10 BILLY. There's plenty of time yet.

11 FLORENCE. Well, she didn't touch none of that salmon, I
      know that. Nobody did. She puts too much out. There's
      some folk would be glad of that. I tell her. . . .

   BILLY *shows some impatience.*

12 GEOFFREY. Course, I don't believe in interfering. You've
      made your mind up. I don't want you to come to me
      and say that I stopped you doing it.

13 BILLY. Well, Dad, it's not that simple. I've not really decided
      what we'll be doing yet.

14 GEOFFREY. You couldn't do no worse than us when we
      started. Me and your mother. We'd nothing—I hadn't
      two ha'pennies to scratch my backside with. We had to
      manage.

15 BILLY. I'm not bothered about managing, Dad. It's just that
      I hadn't made my mind up.

1 GEOFFREY [*almost reverting back to his normal antagonism*]. Well, you want to get your bloody mind made up, lad. Right sharp. Before she does it for you.

2 BILLY. You see . . .

3 FLORENCE [*interrupting*]. I told her. I had my say. I told her, you don't get married till you're twenty-one.

4 BILLY. Just a minute, Grandma . . .

5 FLORENCE [*ignoring him*]. You can do as you like then, I said. Only, I said, don't come running back to me when you can't manage. I said you'll have it to put up with. . . .

6 BILLY [*completely exasperated*]. For Christ's sake belt up!

7 GEOFFREY [*losing his temper completely*] You what! [*He moves across and grabs BILLY by his shirt.*] You what did you say? What was that? What did you say?

8 BILLY [*frightened but unrepentant*]. I merely remarked. . . .

9 GEOFFREY [*shouting*]. Talk bloody properly when you talk to me! You were talking different a minute ago, weren't you? What did you just say to your grandma? What did you just say?

   ALICE *enters from the kitchen.*

10 ALICE. Hey, what's all this row? [*She indicates the kitchen.*] Don't you know we've got somebody here?

11 GEOFFREY. I can't help who's here! She might as well know what he is! Because I'll tell her! [*Shaking him.*] He's ignorant! That's what you are, isn't it? Ignorant! Ignorant! Ignorant! Isn't it?

12 ALICE. Well, don't pull him round. That shirt's clean on.

13 GEOFFREY [*releasing his hold on BILLY*]. I'll clean shirt him before I've finished!

14 ALICE. Well, what's he done?

15 GEOFFREY. I'll clean shirt him round his bloody ear-hole. With his bloody fountain pens and his bloody suède shoes! Well, he doesn't go out tonight. I know where he gets it from. He stops in tonight and tomorrow night as well.

1   BILLY. Look . . .

2   GEOFFREY. Don't 'look' me! With your look this and look
    that! And you can get all that bloody books and
    rubbish or whatever it is cleared out of that sideboard
    cupboard as well! Before I chuck 'em out—and you
    with 'em!

3   BILLY. What's up? They're not hurting you are they?

    BARBARA *enters and stands in the kitchen doorway uncertainly.*

4   GEOFFREY. No, and they're not bloody hurting you either!

5   ALICE [*quietly*]. Well, I don't know what you've done now.

6   GEOFFREY. Answering back at his grandmother. If that's
    what they learned him at grammar school I'm glad I'm
    bloody uneducated! Anyroad, I've finished with him!
    He knows where there's a suitcase. If he wants to go to
    London he can bloody well go.

7   ALICE [*sharply*]. Oh, but he's not.

8   GEOFFREY. I've finished with him. He can go.

9   ALICE. Oh, but he's not.

10 GEOFFREY. He's going! He can get his bloody things together!
    He's going out!

11 ALICE. Oh, but he's not. Oh, but he's not. Oh, but he is not!

12 BILLY [*trying to get a word in*]. Look, can I settle this . . .

13 GEOFFREY [*interrupting*]. It's ever since he started work. Com-
    plaining about this and that and the other. If it isn't his
    boiled eggs it's something else. You have to get special
    bloody wheatflakes for him because there's a bloody
    plastic bloody submarine in the packet. Splashing about
    in the kitchen at his age. He wants putting away. Well,
    I've had enough—he can go.

14 ALICE. Oh, but he's not. Now, you just listen to me, Geoffrey.
    He's not old enough to go to London or anywhere else.

15 GEOFFREY. He's old enough to get himself engaged. He thinks
    he is. He's old enough and bloody daft enough.

1 ALICE. Well, you said yourself. He doesn't think. He gets ideas in his head.

2 GEOFFREY. He can go. I've finished with him.

3 ALICE. Oh, but he is not. Not while I'm here.

4 BARBARA [*who has been staring at* FLORENCE]. Mrs. Fisher . . .

5 GEOFFREY [*ignoring her*]. He wants to get into the bloody army, that's what he wants to do.

6 ALICE [*spiritedly*]. Yes, and you want to get into the bloody army as well.

7 BARBARA. Mrs. Fisher. I don't think Billy's grandma's very well.

ALICE, GEOFFREY *and* BILLY *turn and look at* FLORENCE *who is sitting slumped in her chair.*

8 ALICE [*rushing across to her mother*]. Now look what you've done!

9 GEOFFREY [*to* BILLY]. I hope you're bloody satisfied now. She's had another do.

10 ALICE. It's no use blaming him, Geoffrey. You're both as bad as each other. Well, don't just stand there—get me the smelling salts.

11 BARBARA [*coming forward*]. Can I be doing anything, Mrs. Fisher?

12 ALICE. No . . . no, it's all right. She's getting old, that's all. He'll see to it.

13 GEOFFREY [*crossing to the sideboard he searches through the drawers*]. It's happening too bloody often is this. We can't be having this game every fortnight—neither sense nor reason in it.

14 ALICE. Well, she can't help it, Geoffrey. It's not her fault.

15 GEOFFREY. She'll have to see that bloody doctor. If I've to take time off and take her myself—she'll have to see him.

16 ALICE. She won't see him.

17 GEOFFREY. It's getting past a joke is this. It's not his bloody fault he's a nigger. [*Rifling through a second drawer.*] I wish

you'd keep them salts in the same place. Never here when you want them.

2   ALICE [*patting her mother's wrists*]. Hurry up, Geoffrey!

3   FLORENCE [*who has been slowly coming round during the above begins to mumble*]. I told her about that fire. Banking it up. I get too hot and then I go off. They don't think. Rushing me with my tea.

4   ALICE. It's all right, Mother. You'll be all right.

5   GEOFFREY [*he locates the bottle of smelling salts and crosses and hands them to* ALICE]. Does she want these bloody salts or not?

6   ALICE [*taking the bottle from* GEOFFREY]. She'd better have them. [*She opens the bottle and holds it under* FLORENCE'S *nose.*]

7   FLORENCE. Feathers.

8   GEOFFREY. She's off. She's bloody rambling.

9   FLORENCE. She wants to burn some feathers. Never mind salts. I can't be doing with salts. They make me bilious.

10   ALICE. It's all right, Mother. [*To* GEOFFREY.] We'd better get her upstairs. She's too hot here anyway.

11   GEOFFREY. She'll be too bloody cold if she doesn't see that doctor. It's not fair on us. It's us that has it to put up with.

12   BARBARA. Shall I fetch you a glass of water?

13   ALICE. No—she doesn't have water. She'll be all right in a minute.

14   GEOFFREY. It's happening too regular is this. It's every week alike. And it's always on bloody Saturdays. We can't even sit down to us tea in peace.

15   ALICE. Don't go on at her—you'll only make her worse. Just help me get her off to bed.

16   GEOFFREY [*putting his arm round* FLORENCE *and raising her to her feet. He is gruffly compassionate*]. Come on then, Mother. Let's be having you. She's a bloody ton weight. She puts some weight on for somebody who never eats nothing. [*To* FLORENCE.] You're putting weight on.

17   ALICE. Don't stand there, Billy. Help your father.

1   GEOFFREY [*piloting* FLORENCE *towards the door*]. By bloody hell—
    don't ask him to do nothing. He'll drop her down the
    bedroom stairs.

2   ALICE [*crossing to help him*]. You never give him a chance.

    ALICE *and* GEOFFREY *support* FLORENCE *and move off through the
    hall and up the stairs.*

3   FLORENCE. They ought to put a bed down here . . . Them
    stairs is too steep . . . They could have got the bunga-
    low. . . .

4   GEOFFREY. Now steady . . . Steady on, lass . . . Plenty of time.

    FLORENCE *continues to mumble to herself as they go upstairs. We
    cannot hear what she is saying but one sentence comes out plainly as
    they disappear into the bedroom.*

5   FLORENCE. It's all these blackies. . . .

    In the living-room there is an embarrassed silence between BILLY
    and BARBARA. BILLY *absent-mindedly picks up* FLORENCE'S *hand-
    bag and looks inside it. He goes through the contents idly and takes out
    an obsolete ration book.*

6   BILLY. Do you know, she still keeps her old ration book?

7   BARBARA. I noticed she didn't look very well. Even at tea-
    time. I noticed but I didn't like to say anything.

8   BILLY [*after a pause*]. You wouldn't think she'd been all over
    the world, would you? Paris—Cairo—Vienna.

9   BARBARA [*incredulously*]. Who? Your grandma?

10 BILLY. My grandad was in the Diplomatic Corps. Before he
    had his leg off. He could speak seven languages, you
    know. They went all over.

11 BARBARA [*completely disbelieving him she decides to ignore this state-
    ment*]. Do you think your mother's going to like me, pet?

12 BILLY. He was in the French Foreign Legion for nine years.

13 BARBARA. I think we should get on with each other. It's better
    when you do—really. When families stick together.
    Why didn't you tell them we'd got engaged?

1   BILLY. I was going to. Did you show them the ring?

2   BARBARA [*examining the ring*]. Of course. I show it to everybody. It's lovely. I won't be completely happy until I've got the other one to go with it.

3   BILLY. Darling . . . [*Taking her hand.*] You will always love me, won't you?

4   BARBARA. You know I will.

5   BILLY [*his fingers on the engagement ring*]. I still say this ring's too big. Why won't you let me get it altered?

6   BARBARA [*pulling her hand away*]. I don't think it's too big. Anyway, I want everybody to see it first.

7   BILLY. Well, don't blame me if you lose it. My mother was saying it was nearly coming off while you were washing up. It'll only take a couple of days. And then it'll be there for ever. [*Romantically.*] For ever and ever. . . .

8   BARBARA. Sweet . . .

9   BILLY. So go on, then. Give me it. You can have it back on Wednesday.

10   BARBARA. No, I'll never take it off. Never—never.

11   BILLY. Give me the cowing ring!

12   BARBARA. Billy!

13   BILLY [*moving away from her in disgust*]. Oh, please yourself, then. Don't say I didn't warn you.

RITA *approaches the house through the garden. She is a small girl with blonde hair—seventeen years old but she dresses to look much older. She is common and hard and works in a snack bar.*

14   BARBARA. Now you're cross. Don't be, pet. I'll take care of it. And I'll never lose it.

RITA *rings the bell.*

15   BILLY. Just a minute.

He crosses into the hall and opens the front door.

Rita!

1 RITA [*moving forward menacingly*]. Right, I suppose you . . .

2 BILLY [*interrupting her*]. Just a minute!

    He slams the door on RITA *and moves across the hall to speak to*
    BARBARA.

    Just a minute! [*He closes the living-room door.*]

3 ALICE [*appearing at the top of the staircase*]. Who is it, Billy?

4 BILLY. Just a minute!

    BILLY *opens the front door and enters the garden, closing the door*
    behind him.

    BARBARA *takes an orange from her handbag and is peeling it as the*
    lights fade down on the living-room and the lights come up on the
    garden set.

    Hello, Rita.

5 RITA [*her conversation consists mainly of clichés and expressions picked up*
    on amorous evenings spent with friendly American airmen]. Ooh!
    Look what's crawled out of the cheese!

6 BILLY. Hello, Rita—sorry I can't ask you in.

7 RITA. Get back in the knife-box, big-head.

8 BILLY. We're flooded. The pipes have burst.

9 RITA. Are you kidding? Here, pull the other one—it's got
    bells on it.

10 BILLY. What's the matter, darling? Is anything wrong?

11 RITA. Hark at Lord Muck. Don't come the innocent with
    me. You know what's wrong. I thought you were
    going to your uncle's on Wednesday night.

12 BILLY. I did go to my uncle's. My Uncle Herbert's.

13 RITA. Well, you didn't then—because somebody saw you.
    Sitting in the Gaumont. With your arm round a lass
    eating oranges.

14 BILLY. They didn't see me. I was at my Uncle Ernest's playing
    Monopoly.

1   RITA [*imitating him*]. At my Uncle Ernest's playing Monopoly. You rotten liar! You're just muck. You're rotten, that's what you are. And where's my engagement ring?

2   BILLY. I'm glad you asked me that question. Because I called into the shop this morning and the man said it might be another week.

3   RITA [*again imitating him*]. The man said it might be another week. You're worse than muck. You're rotten.

4   BILLY. No, because they can't do it up here. They've got to send it to Bradford. They've got three people off ill.

5   RITA [*again imitating him*]. Three people off ill. Yes, I suppose they're all having their legs off. To hear you talk everybody's having their leg off. And another thing, I thought I was coming round for my tea this afternoon. To meet your rotten mother.

6   BILLY. Yes, darling, but something happened. My grandma was taken ill. Last Thursday. They've got her in bed.

7   RITA. Well, I am going to see your rotten mother—I'll tell you that. My name's not 'Silly', you know. Either you get me that rotten ring back or I'm going to see your rotten mother.

8   BILLY [*attempting to quieten her*]. Sssh, darling!

9   RITA [*raising her voice*]. And your rotten father! And your rotten grandmother!

In a wild attempt to quieten RITA, BILLY *takes her in his arms and kisses her. She responds with an automatic animal passion. They break away.*

You are rotten to me, Billy. I'm not kidding, you know. I still want that ring back. [*Her voice rises again.*] And my dad wants to know where it is as well. We're supposed to be engaged, you know.

10   BILLY. You once said you didn't want to marry me.

11   RITA. Don't come that tale with me. I said I didn't want to live in a rotten cottage in Devon—that's all.

1 BILLY. We'll live wherever you like, darling. Nothing matters as long as we're together.

2 RITA. Well, can you get it back tonight, then?

3 BILLY. Of course I can, darling. If that's what you want. [*He kisses her again.*] Darling, darling, darling.

4 RITA [*pushing* BILLY *away as his hand creeps round her back*]. Hey, Bolton Wanderer! Keep your mucky hands to yourself.

5 BILLY. Tell me you're not cross with me, darling.

6 RITA [*imitating him*]. Tell me you're not cross . . . Put another record on, we've heard that one. And get that ring back.

7 BILLY. I will. I promise, darling. I'll go down to the shop. I'll give it to you tonight—at the dance.

8 RITA. You'd better do—or else there'll be bother. I wouldn't like to be in your shoes if my father comes round. And he will, you know. And he won't stand arguing in the garden. [BILLY *kisses her again.*] Go on, then. Go in and get your coat on—and get off for that ring.

9 BILLY. See you tonight, darling.

10 RITA. Never mind see you tonight, shops'll be shut in half an hour. You'll get off now. Go on, then, get your coat. You can walk me down as far as the bus-stop. Go on, Dateless, don't stand there catching flies.

11 BILLY. I can't go yet.

12 RITA. Why not? What's stopping you?

13 BILLY. I'm waiting to go to the lavatory. My mam's on.

14 RITA. I'll be walking on. You catch me up.

    RITA *walks off, slowly, down the garden and goes.* BILLY *enters the house. As he crosses through the hall the lights fade down in the garden and come up in the living-room.* BARBARA *is just finishing eating the orange.*

15 BILLY. Hey, listen! I've just had my fortune told by a gipsy.

16 BARBARA. I've eaten a whole orange while I've been waiting.

17 BILLY. She says there's a curse on me.

1   BARBARA. Your mother's not come down yet. Neither has your father.

2   BILLY. I'm going to experience sorrow and misfortune but after a long journey things will start to go right. Hey, she had a baby on her back like a Red Indian.

3   BARBARA. Do you think she'll be all right—your grand-mother?

BILLY *crosses and sits in the armchair.*

4   BILLY. Who? Oh, my grandma! Yes, she'll be all right. It's just that she's got this rare disease—they're trying a new drug out on her.

5   BARBARA. She looked as though she was having some kind of fit at first. I noticed when you were having that row with your father.

6   BILLY. They've only tried it out three times—this drug. Once on President Eisenhower, then the Duke of Windsor and then my grandma.

7   BARBARA. Honestly! No wonder your father gets cross with you.

8   BILLY. How do you mean?

9   BARBARA. Well, all these stories you keep telling—no wonder he keeps losing his temper.

10 BILLY. Oh, you don't take any notice of him.

11 BARBARA. Billy?

12 BILLY. What?

13 BARBARA. What was your father saying? About you going to London?

14 BILLY. Did he? When? I never heard him.

15 BARBARA. When he was talking about answering back at your grandmother. When he got hold of your shirt. He said, 'If you want to go to London you can "B" well go'. He swore.

16 BILLY. I know. He's been summonsed twice for using bad language.

1 BARBARA. Yes, but what did he mean?

2 BILLY. What? About going to London?

3 BARBARA. Yes.

4 BILLY. Ah, well—there's a very interesting story behind that.

5 BARBARA. No, Billy, this is important—to us. You've got to think about me now.

6 BILLY (*he rises and crosses towards her*]. It's for you I'm doing it, my darling.

7 BARBARA. What do you mean?

8 BILLY [*sitting down beside her and taking her hand he goes off into a fantasy*]. Isn't it obvious? How can we go on living like this?

9 BARBARA [*automatically freeing her hand she takes an orange from her handbag*]. What do you mean, pet? Like what?

10 BILLY. In this—this atmosphere. Do you honestly think that we could ever be happy—I mean really happy—here?

11 BARBARA. Where?

12 BILLY. In this house. There's the shadow of my father across this house. He's a bitter man, Barbara.

13 BARBARA [*she settles down and begins to peel the orange*]. Why? What for? What about?

14 BILLY. He's jealous. Every time he looks at me he sees his own hopes and the failure of his own ambitions.

15 BARBARA. Your father?

16 BILLY. He had his dreams once. He can't bear it—seeing me on the brink of success. He was going to be a writer too.

17 BARBARA. Billy, if this is going to be another of your stories . . .

18 BILLY. You don't have to believe me. The evidence is here—in this house.

19 BARBARA. Evidence? How do you mean—evidence?

20 BILLY [*pointing to the sideboard*]. It's all in there.

21 BARBARA. What is?

1   BILLY. Go and look for yourself. In that cupboard.

> BARBARA *rises and crosses to the sideboard. She tugs at the handle on* BILLY'S *cupboard.*

2   BARBARA. It's locked.

3   BILLY [*meaningly*]. Yes.

4   BARBARA. Where's the key?

5   BILLY. God knows. I was four years old when that was locked, Barbara. It's never been opened since.

6   BARBARA [*crossing towards* BILLY]. Well, what's supposed to be in it?

7   BILLY. Hopes! Dreams! Ambitions! The life work of a disillusioned man. Barbara, there must be forty or fifty unpublished novels in that cupboard. All on the same bitter theme.

8   BARBARA [*in half-belief*]. Well, we can't all be geniuses.

9   BILLY. Perhaps not. But he crucified himself in the attempt. Sitting night after night at that table. Chewing at his pen. And when the words wouldn't come he'd take it out on us.

10 BARBARA. But what about going to London? What about our cottage in Devon?

> ALICE *emerges from the bedroom and comes down the stairs.*

11 BILLY. Well, it's all down south, Barbara. We could live in the New Forest. We could have a cottage there—a woodman's cottage—in a clearing.

12 BARBARA. I think I'd be frightened. Living in a forest.

13 BILLY [*he puts his arm round her*]. Not with me to look after you, you wouldn't.

> BILLY *rises awkwardly as* ALICE *enters the room.* ALICE *is faintly preoccupied. She crosses towards the kitchen and speaks almost to herself.*

44

1   ALICE. Well, she seems to be resting.

ALICE goes into the kitchen. There is a slight feeling of embarrass-ment between BILLY *and* BARBARA *and then* BARBARA *speaks to break the silence.*

2   BARBARA. Are we going out dancing tonight?

3   BILLY. If you like . . . [*He claps his hand to his forehead in an over-dramatic gesture.*) Oh, no! Just remembered!

4   BARBARA [*suspiciously*]. What?

5   BILLY. I promised to go round to my Uncle Herbert's tonight. To play Monopoly. It's his birthday.

6   BARBARA. Funny you never told me before. You're always having to go round to your Uncle Herbert's. Anyway, I thought it was your Uncle Ernest who played Mono-poly?

7   BILLY. Ah, well . . . I'm glad you asked me that question. You see, my Uncle Herbert. . . .

8   BARBARA [*interrupting*]. Oh, don't bother. You and your relatives. If I didn't know you better I'd think you had another girl.

9   BILLY. Darling! What a thing to say!

10 BARBARA. You know that Liz is back in town, don't you?

11 BILLY. Liz who?

12 BARBARA. You know who. That dirty girl. I'm surprised you weren't ashamed to be seen with her.

13 BILLY. Oh, her . . . I haven't seen her for donkeys years.

ALICE enters from the kitchen. She is carrying a tumbler containing a white liquid which she is stirring with a spoon.

14 ALICE. Her breathing's all right—she's still awake, though. I think she'd be better if we could get her off to sleep.

15 BARBARA. She was looking tired this afternoon.

16 ALICE [*gently reprimanding*]. Well, I blame you as much as any-body. You set your father off and then it sets her off. I've told you time and time again.

1 BILLY [*half-ashamed*]. She's all right now, is she, then?

2 ALICE. Is she ever all right?

3 BARBARA. Are you quite sure there's nothing I can do? could she eat an orange?

4 ALICE. I'm going to get the doctor in to her—be on the safe side. Whether she wants him or not. Your father's sitting with her. [*She hands* BILLY *the tumbler.*] Can you take this up without spilling it?

5 BILLY [*taking the tumbler reluctantly*]. Who? Me?

6 ALICE. Either that or ring the doctor up for me. [*Rather impatiently.*] But do something, lad, don't just stand there.

> ALICE *turns away from him and walks briskly into the hall where she picks up the phone.* BILLY *stands indecisively for a moment and then crosses through into the hall and up the stairs as* ALICE *dials the number. She waits for a reply and glances up at* BILLY *who has, for no reason at all, developed a limp. She calls up to him.*

Now, what are you playing at!

> BILLY *stops limping and quickens his pace and goes into the bedroom as* ALICE *turns back to the phone.*

Hello, is that the surgery? . . . Well, it's Mrs. Fisher, forty-two Park Drive . . . Yes, that's right. Only it's my mother again. Mrs. Boothroyd. Do you think the doctor could call round? . . . Oh, dear. Only we've got her in bed again . . . I've given her her tablets—and the mixture . . . Well, will you ask him to come round as soon as he can? . . . Yes, yes, I will, I will—thank you very much. Good-bye.

> ALICE *replaces the phone and crosses into the living-room.*

You don't like to bother them on a Saturday but what else can you do?

7 BARBARA. Is the doctor coming, Mrs. Fisher?

8 ALICE. He's coming sometime—when he's ready. It'll be nine o'clock again, I suppose. He's already out on his calls.

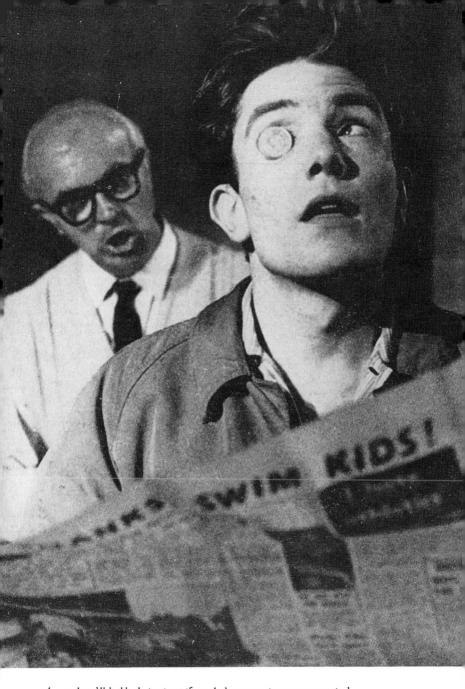

'... *and you'll be bloody imminent if you don't start getting up on a morning*'

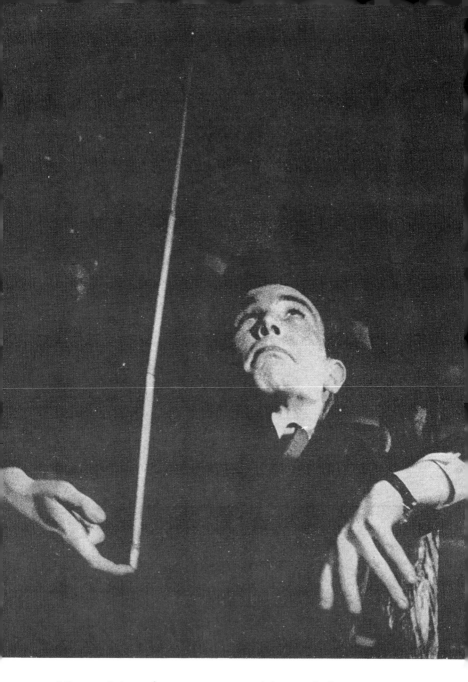

Billy toys with the cane for a moment, attempting to balance it on his finger

Liz

Barbara

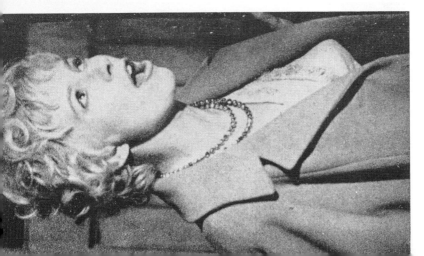

Rita

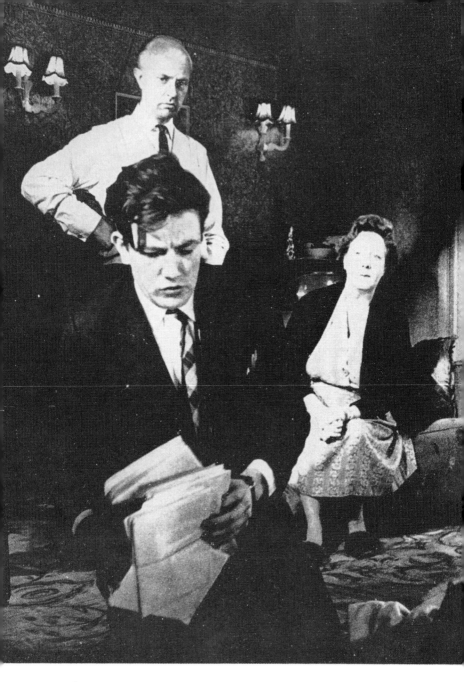

'What the thump are you packing them bloody calendars for?'

1 BARBARA. I shouldn't worry. He'll be round as soon as he can.

2 ALICE [sitting]. You can't help worrying sometimes. If I don't worry nobody else will. It's just getting me down, is this. It's just one thing after another.

3 BARBARA [returns to her seat on the couch and takes up the orange]. Would you like a piece of orange, Mrs. Fisher?

4 ALICE [she looks up and, for the first time, realizes that BARBARA is trying to help]. No. No, thank you. Not just at this minute, love. Thank you.

5 BARBARA. Would it be better if I went? [Half-rising.] I mean if I'm in the way.

6 ALICE. No, don't be silly. You sit yourself down. I'm only sorry it's happened while you were here.

7 BARBARA [returning to her seat]. You can't arrange illness, can you?

8 ALICE. You can't. I only wish you could. Only she has these turns and all you can do is put her to bed. But she always seems to pick the most awkward times. Still, you can't blame her. It's not her fault. You might think it is to hear him talk. You'd think she does it on purpose, to listen to him.

9 BARBARA. She might be better before the doctor comes.

10 ALICE. It wears me out, I know that. And if it isn't her it's our Billy. I don't know what we're going to do with him.

11 BARBARA. I think he wants to help—but he doesn't like to offer.

12 ALICE. He didn't use to be like this. He's got to grow up sometime. I don't know, it might be better if he did go to London. It might put some sense into him if he had to look after himself.

13 BARBARA. Well, that's what I don't understand, Mrs. Fisher. Is he going to London?

14 ALICE. Well, he reckons he is. Hasn't he said anything to you?

47

1 BARBARA. Well, not really. I only heard what his father said. I tried to ask him.

2 ALICE. What did he say to you?

3 BARBARA. Nothing, really. [*She indicates the sideboard.*] He just started talking about that cupboard.

4 ALICE. Oh, don't talk to me about that cupboard. I don't know what he keeps in there. I'm frightened to ask, to tell you the honest truth.

5 BARBARA. He said it had been locked since he was four years old.

6 ALICE. I don't know why he says these things. I mean, what good does it do him? It's not as if he gets anything out of it.

7 BARBARA. I'm quite sure I don't know. He told me Mr. Fisher was a captain on a petrol ship.

8 ALICE. Don't let his father hear you say that—else there'll be trouble. He'll murder him one of these days. If he knew all I know he'd have murdered him long ago. I could do it myself sometimes. And he says things we can find out about, that's what I don't understand. He told me that young lad who works in the fruit shop had gassed himself—and he knows I go in there every Tuesday.

9 BARBARA. I know. He says all kinds of things.

10 ALICE. I don't know where he'll end up—it's not our fault, I do know that. We've done our best for him. His father says it's since he started work—but I know different. It's ever since he went to that grammar school. He wanted to go, so we let him—he'd not been there five minutes before he wanted to leave. And we had it all to pay for, you know—he never appreciated it. School uniform, he loses his cap first week. Cricketing trousers, he never wore them. We bought him a satchel and he let a lad run away with it. Then there was his books to pay for— well, he never reads them. It's just been a waste of time and money. You'd think he'd been dragged up. He's not cleaned his shoes for six months.

1   BARBARA. I tell him about his shoes. He takes no notice. And his hair—he won't have a haircut, will he?

2   ALICE. Well, he doesn't take after me—or his father. And it's us that's got to clean up after him. He got them suède shoes so he wouldn't have to bother cleaning them— but you can't just not touch them. He trod in some dog-dirt on Tuesday and—do you know?—he walked it round this house for three days. I had to get a knife and scrape it off myself, in the finish. [*Distastefully, recalling the incident.*] Pooh! You could smell it all over the house.

3   BARBARA. My mother won't have a dog. And she hates cats.

4   ALICE. You can't keep on telling him—it just goes in one ear and out the other. He wants watching all the time, that's his trouble. You see, if he'd gone into the business with his father, like we wanted him to, we could have kept an eye on him more. But he won't listen. He went after all kinds of daft jobs. That lady in the Juvenile Employment Bureau, she lost patience with him. He wouldn't have this and he wouldn't have that. And she offered him some lovely jobs to begin with. He could have gone as a junior trainee at the Co-op Bank if he'd wanted to. She offered him that.

5   BARBARA. I know somebody who works there, she likes it. They've got their own social club.

6   ALICE. She just stopped bothering. She couldn't get any sense out of him. She asked him what he did want in the end and he told her he wanted to be either a merchant seaman or a concert pianist. Grammar school! You'd think he'd been to the Silly School. He shows me up.

7   BARBARA. How did he come to work for Shadrack and Duxbury's?

8   ALICE. Don't ask me. He'd been left school a fortnight and he was still no nearer a job—he wanted to work in the museum by this time. We were sick and tired of having him lounging about the house. His father comes home

one morning at twelve o'clock and finds him playing with some Plasticine. He went mad. He told him straight out. He says, you get out of this house, and get yourself a job, my lad, he says. And, he says, don't you dare come back without one—or I'll knock your blooming head right off your shoulders—only he didn't say blooming.

2　BARBARA. No, I can imagine.

3　ALICE. So, of course, our Billy goes out and waltzes back two hours later and says he's working for an undertaker—start on Monday. He's been there ever since.

4　BARBARA. I don't think he likes it, though, does he?

5　ALICE. Like it or lump it, he's got to work for his living. Never mind going to London. He's got no mind of his own, that's his trouble. He listens to these pals he's got. What they do he's got to do. I'm only glad he's found himself a sensible lass, for once.

BILLY *emerges from the bedroom and comes down the stairs.*

6　BARBARA. I think it was that girl he used to go about with before he met me, Mrs. Fisher. That funny girl. That Liz. She used to put a lot of ideas into his head.

BILLY *pauses at the foot of the stairs and listens to their conversation.*

7　ALICE. Oh, that one. I've seen him with her. She looked as though a good bath wouldn't do her any harm. I don't know what kind of a family she comes from. I'm only glad she's gone.

8　BARBARA. She's come back again, didn't you know? She goes off all over, all the time. By herself. I don't think she's got any family. Do you know what I don't like about her, Mrs. Fisher? She smokes and she keeps her cigarette in her mouth when she's talking. I could never do that. It looks common.

9　ALICE. You could always tell when he'd been out with her. The ideas he used to come home with. He comes home one night and says he wants to go off on holiday with

her. To the Norfolk Broads, if you like. I told him—
straight. I said, that's not the way we do things in this
house. I said, if you want to go on holiday you can come
to Morecambe with us—and if you don't you can stop
at home.

2 BARBARA. I don't believe in mixed holidays—not before
you're married.

3 ALICE. I'm sure you don't, love. You wouldn't be sitting here
if you did, I can tell you.

4 BARBARA. He was saying you wouldn't mind if I went to
Blackpool with him for a week—but I wouldn't. I don't
believe in anything like that.

5 ALICE. He was saying what!

  BILLY *enters hastily and changes the subject.*

6 BILLY. Hey, listen! [ALICE *and* BARBARA *turn to* BILLY *who is trying to
think of something to say next. He tries in desperation to joke.*]
Fifteen men under one umbrella and not one of them
got wet. [*He evokes no reaction.*] It wasn't raining.

7 ALICE [*to* BARBARA]. Well, you can't say you don't know what
you're letting yourself in for. [*To* BILLY.] Stop acting so
daft with people poorly. We've got enough on our
plates without you.

8 BARBARA. How's your grandma, Billy? Is she any better?

9 ALICE. Has she gone off to sleep yet?

10 BILLY. She looks all right to me.

11 ALICE. Is your father all right with her? Would he like me to
go up? Does he want anything?

12 BILLY. I don't know.

13 ALICE. No, and I don't suppose you care. [*Losing her temper.*]
Have you had a wash since you got up this morning?

14 BILLY. Course I have.

15 ALICE. Yes, a cat-lick. I bet you didn't take your shirt off, did
you? You'll have to smarten your idea up, you know,
if you want to go script-writing. They don't have them

on the B.B.C. with mucky necks. You'll start washing your own shirts in future, I can't get them clean.

2　BILLY [*acutely embarrassed but, for* BARBARA'S *benefit, he pretends to be amused and winds an imaginary* gramophone *handle*]. Crikey Moses, she's off!

3　BARBARA. Well, you can't say you've had a shave this morning, Billy, because you haven't.

4　BILLY. I'm growing a beard, if you want to know.

5　ALICE. Oh no, you're not. We're having no beards in this house.

6　BARBARA. I don't think I'd like you with a beard, Billy.

7　ALICE. He's not having a beard.

8　BILLY. I'm having a bloody beard.

9　ALICE. Hey, hey, hey! Language! Don't you start coming out with that talk! Else you'll get a shock coming, big as you are! We get enough of that from your father.

10　BILLY. Well, I'm still having a beard. I can grow one in six weeks.

11　BARBARA. I don't think you should, Billy. Not if your mother doesn't want you to.

12　ALICE. He's got no say in the matter. If I say he doesn't grow a beard, he doesn't grow one.

13　BILLY. What's up with you? It's my stinking face!

14　ALICE. I'll not tell you again about that language! You can start to alter yourself, that's what you can do, my lad. We're not going on like this for much longer. Either brighten your ideas up or do as your father says—and get off to London or where you like. Because we're not going on like this, day in and day out! It's not fair on nobody!

15　BILLY. Oh, shut up!

16　ALICE. And you can start watching what you say to people, as well. What did you say to me about that lad in the fruit shop? Gassing himself? And what have you been telling Barbara about that cupboard?

1   BILLY. What cupboard?

2   ALICE. You know very well what cupboard!

3   BILLY. I don't know what cupboard. How do you mean—cupboard?

4   BARBARA. Your sideboard cupboard.

5   BILLY. What about it?

6   BARBARA. That evidence you were talking about. In the cupboard. When you were four years old. All these unpublished novels. Where your father was chewing his pen up.

7   BILLY. Oh, that! Oh, you should have said. No, you're getting mixed up. I was talking about his invoices that he writes out. He keeps them in that vase—I didn't say anything about any cupboard.

8   BARBARA [shocked]. Billy Fisher! I don't know how you can stand there! He'll be struck down dead one of these days.

9   BILLY [with a pretence at innocence]. What's up?

10   ALICE. He can stand there as if butter wouldn't melt in his mouth.

11   BILLY. I don't know what you're all on about.

12   BARBARA. Oh yes, you do. Don't try and make it out as if it's me, Billy.

13   BILLY. It is you. Look—Barbara—you were sitting over there, weren't you? On that couch. Because you were eating an orange. And I was standing over there. Right? It is right, isn't it? You were sitting there and I was standing there.

14   BARBARA. Yes, but then you said your father. . . .

15   ALICE. Never mind what he said, love, I know what he is.

     RITA *enters the garden and stands, for a moment, hesitantly outside the front door.*

16   BILLY. Yes, you'll believe her, won't you?

1　ALICE. I'd believe anybody before you, Billy. I'm very sorry, but there it is. I'd believe Hitler before I'd believe you.

2　BILLY. Why don't you come straight out and call me a liar, then!

3　ALICE. Well, you are one. I don't care who knows it.

4　BILLY. Well, that's a nice thing for a mother to say, isn't it?

5　ALICE. Yes, and you're a nice son for a mother to have, aren't you? You don't think what you're doing to me, do you? You never consider anybody except yourself.

6　BILLY. I suppose you do, don't you?

7　ALICE. Yes, I do. I worry about you, I know that.

8　BILLY. Well, what about me? Don't you think I worry? I worry about the H-bomb. You didn't know I nearly went on the Aldermaston march last Easter, did you? I don't want another war, you know. And what about all them refugees? You never stop to consider them, do you? Or South Africa.

At this point RITA *makes up her mind, and, without knocking, marches into the house and into the living-room.*

Do you know, Barbara, if you were a blackie and we lived in South Africa I'd be in gaol by now? Doing fifteen years. [*At which point he breaks off as* RITA *makes her entrance.*] Hallo, Rita.

9　RITA [*to* BILLY, *indicating* ALICE]. It takes her some time to come out of the lavatory, doesn't it? What's she been doing? Writing her will out?

10　ALICE [*outraged*]. Do you usually come into people's houses without knocking?

11　RITA. I do when people have got my private property. [*To* BILLY.] Come on—give.

12　BILLY. Rita, I don't think you've ever met my mother, have you?

13　RITA. No, but she'll know me again, won't she? Come on, you and your stinking rotten jewellers. I'm not daft, you know.

1   ALICE [*shocked*]. We're not having this! Where does she think she is?

2   BILLY [*attempting to guide* RITA *towards the door he takes her elbow*]. I'll just take Rita as far as the bus stop, mother.

3   RITA [*shrugging him away*]. Take your mucky hands off me, you rotten toffee-nosed get. You didn't think I'd come in, did you?

4   ALICE. No, but I think you'll go out, young lady. And if you've anything to say to my son you'd better just remember where you are.

5   BILLY. Well, I'm very glad you have come, Rita, because I feel I owe you a word of explanation.

6   RITA [*imitating him*]. Oooh, I feel I owe you a word of explanation. Get back in the cheese, with the other maggots.

7   ALICE. I'm not putting up with this—I shall bring his father down.

8   RITA. You can bring his rotten father down. I hope you do. And his rotten grandma.

9   BARBARA. Billy's grandma, for your information, happens to be ill in bed.

10   RITA [*turning to* BARBARA *for the first time*]. Oooh, look what the cat's brought in. Get Madam Fancy-knickers. I suppose this is your rotten sister. I thought she was supposed to be in a rotten iron lung.

11   BARBARA. For your information, I happen to be Billy's fiancée.

12   RITA [*imitating* BARBARA]. Oooh, for your information. Well, for your information, he happens to be engaged to me. In front of a witness.

13   BILLY. How do you mean? What's witnesses got to do with it?

14   BARBARA. Billy, will you kindly tell me who this girl is?

15   RITA [*imitating her*]. Oooh, Billy, will you kindly tell me? Aw, go take a long walk on a short pier, you squint-eyed sow, you're nothing else.

1 ALICE. Barbara, would you kindly go upstairs and ask Mr. Fisher to come down for a minute?

2 RITA. You can fetch him down. Fetch all the rotten lot down. You can fetch the cowing iron lung down as well, for all I care.

3 ALICE. I've never been spoken to like this in all my days.

4 BARBARA. Shall I go up, Mrs. Fisher?

5 RITA [*imitating her*]. Oooh, shall I go up, Mrs. Fisher? If you can get up the stairs with them bow legs, you can.

6 ALICE. It's all right, Barbara. I'll deal with this young madam. I've met her type before.

7 BILLY. I think I can explain all this.

8 BARBARA. Yes, I think you've got some explaining to do, Billy.

9 RITA. He can explain until he's blue in the rotten face. It makes no difference to me.

10 ALICE. If I knew your mother, young lady, wouldn't I have something to say to her.

11 RITA. You can keep out of this. It's between me and him. [*To* BILLY.] Where's my ring? Has she got it? [BARBARA's *right hand instinctively goes to her left.*] She has, hasn't she? You've given it to her, haven't you?

12 BILLY. Ah, well—yes, but you see . . . Only there's been a bit of a mix-up. You see, I thought Barbara had broken the engagement off.

13 BARBARA. Billy!

14 RITA. Yeh, well you've got another think coming if you think I'm as daft as she is. You gave that ring to me. And don't think you can go crawling out of it, 'cause you can't. You seem to forget I've got a witness, you know. I've got two. 'Cause Shirley Mitchem saw you giving me it, as well—so you needn't think she didn't. I can go down to the Town Hall, you know.

15 ALICE. Now, don't you come running in here with them tales, my girl. You know as well as I do he's under-age.

1 RITA. Ask him if he was under-age down at Foley Bottoms last night. 'Cause I'm not carrying the can back for nobody. He wasn't under-age then. He was over-age more like.

2 ALICE. Get out! Get out of my house!

3 BARBARA. Have you been untrue to me, Billy? I've got to know.

4 RITA [*imitating her*]. Oooh, have you been untrue to me, Billy! Get out of your push-chair, babyface. [*To* BILLY.] You're just rotten, aren't you? You are—you're rotten, all through. I've met some people in my time, but of all the lying, scheming . . . anyway, you gave that ring to me.

5 BILLY. Yes, but, look, Rita . . .

6 RITA [*interrupting*]. Don't talk to me, you rotten get. Well, she can have you—if she knows what to do with you, which I very much doubt. You rotten lying get. Garr—you think you're somebody, don't you? But you're nobody. You miserable lying rotten stinking get.

7 BILLY. Does this mean you're breaking off our engagement?

8 RITA. You don't get out of it like that. I want that ring.

9 BARBARA [*finding the right word at last*]. Billy, have you been—having relations with this girl?

10 RITA [*swinging round on* BARBARA]. What do you think he's been doing? Knitting a pullover? You know what you can do, don't you. You can give me that ring. Because it's mine.

11 ALICE. If you don't stop it this minute! [*To* BILLY.] As for you, I hope you know what you've done, because I don't.

12 RITA. Are you going to give me that ring?

13 BARBARA. I shall give the ring back to Billy—if and when I break off the engagement.

14 BILLY [*moving towards her*]. Barbara.

15 RITA. Yes, you can go to her. She can have you. And she knows what she can do, the squint-eyed, bow-legged, spotty, snotty-nosed streak of nothing.

1 BARBARA. And you know what you can do as well. You can
   wash your mouth out with soap and water.

2 RITA [*imitating*]. Oooh, you can wash your mouth out with
   soap and water. You could do with some soap in your
   ears, you've got carrots growing out of them. Well, you
   can give me that ring. Before I come over there and get
   it.

3 ALICE. You can get out of this house. I won't tell you again.

4 RITA. Save your breath for blowing out candles. I want my
   ring. [*Crossing towards* BARBARA.] Yes, and I'm going to get
   it.

5 ALICE. Get out of my house! Get out! Get out!

   GEOFFREY FISHER *emerges from the bedroom and comes slowly
   down the stairs.*

6 RITA [*moving right up to* BARBARA]. Are you going to give me that
   ring, or aren't you?

7 GEOFFREY [*half-way down the stairs*]. Mother! . . . Mother!

8 RITA. Because you'll be in Emergency Ward Ten if I don'
   get it—right sharpish.

9 BARBARA. Don't you threaten me.

10 RITA. I won't threaten you—I'll flatten you! Give me that
   cowing ring back! [*She makes a grab for* BARBARA'S *hand.*]

11 BARBARA [*pushing her away*]. I won't . . . I won't. . . .

12 ALICE. Will you stop it, the pair of you!

   GEOFFREY *enters the room and stands in the doorway. He appears not
   to comprehend what is happening.*

13 GEOFFREY. Mother!

   GEOFFREY'S *word silences* ALICE, BILLY *and* BARBARA *who turn
   and look at him.*

14 RITA [*unconcerned*]. Give me the ring!

15 GEOFFREY. You'd better come upstairs. Come now. I think
   she's dead.

   THE CURTAIN FALLS

Act 3

It is about half-past nine the same evening and quite dark in the garden outside
the FISHERS' house. When the action of the play takes place in the garden,
however, a street lamp comes up from the road beyond the garden and off-stage.
There is also a small light in the porch of the house. As the curtain rises
GEOFFREY FISHER is going through the contents of BILLY'S cupboard which are,
at the moment, spread across the floor of the living-room by the sideboard.
ALICE FISHER is sitting in a chair by the fire. She is obviously distraught by the
death of her mother. GEOFFREY rummages through the envelopes and papers and
then rises, shaking his head.

1   GEOFFREY. Well, I can't bloody find it. It's not in here, any-
       way. He hasn't got it. It's about the only bloody thing
       he hasn't got.

2   ALICE. She might not have had one, Geoffrey—you know
       what she was like.

3   GEOFFREY [although he hasn't changed his vocabulary there is a more
       tender note than usual in his voice]. Don't talk so bloody wet,
       lass. Everybody's got a birth certificate.

4   ALICE. Well, you don't know, Geoffrey, they might not have
       had them in those days. She was getting on.

5   GEOFFREY. Everybody's got a bloody birth certificate. They've
       had them since the year dot. If he's got it squat some-
       where I'll bloody mark him for life.

6   ALICE. You can't blame our Billy for everything, Geoffrey.
       What would he want with it?

7   GEOFFREY [indicating the papers on the floor]. What's he want with
       this bloody lot? There's neither sense nor bloody
       reason in him. And where is he, anyway? Where's he
       taken himself off to?

8   ALICE. I don't know, Geoffrey. I've given up caring.

9   GEOFFREY. You'd think he could stay in one bloody night of
       the year. He ought to be in tonight. He ought to be in

looking after his mother. He's got no sense of bloody responsibility, that's his trouble.

2 ALICE. Well, she liked her cup of tea. We'll have that pint-pot to put away now. She's used that pint-pot for as long as I can remember.

3 GEOFFREY. She liked her bloody tea, there's no getting away from it. [*He half-jokes in an attempt to lift* ALICE *out of her depression.*] If I had a shilling for every pot of tea she's supped I'd be a rich man today. Well, there's one good thing to be said for it, when does the dustbin man come around?' Cause he can take all them tins of condensed milk out of her bedroom.

4 ALICE. We can't throw them away. Somebody might be glad of them. We could send them round to the Old People's Home, or something.

5 GEOFFREY. Get away with you, you'd poison the bloody lot of them. That stuff doesn't keep for ever you know. They'll be green mouldy.

6 ALICE. I thought it was supposed to keep—condensed milk.

7 GEOFFREY. It won't keep twenty bloody years, I'm sure. She's had that pile of tins stacked up there since nineteen thirty-nine. And there's not one of them been opened —not one.

8 ALICE. Well, they went scarce, Geoffrey, when the war started, you know. That's why she started saving them.

9 GEOFFREY. Went scarce? Too bloody true they went scarce, she had them all. She hoarded them—she was like a squirrel with them. If Lord Woolton had heard about her in nineteen forty-one she'd have got fifteen years. By bloody hell, she would. [*He reminisces gently.*] Hey! I say! Do you remember how I used to pull her leg about it? How I used to tell her the Food Office was ringing up for her? You couldn't get her near that bloody telephone. She used to let it ring when we were out—she must have lost me pounds.

10 ALICE [*not cheered by* GEOFFREY's *attempt at humour*]. Well, I only hope you manage as well when you're as old as she

was. She's not had an easy life—I wish I could have made it easier for her. She had all us to bring up, you know. And that took some doing.

2   GEOFFREY. No—she didn't do too bad, to say. What was she? Eighty-what?

3   ALICE. She'd have been eighty-three in August. Either eighty-three or eighty-two. She didn't seem to know herself.

4   GEOFFREY. Well, I shan't grumble if I last as long—she had a fair old crack of the whip.

5   ALICE. She didn't suffer, that's something to be grateful for. Some of them hang on for months and months. What did you say she was talking about? Before she went?

6   GEOFFREY. Don't ask me. I couldn't hear for that bloody shambles that was going on down here. I've never heard anything like it in all my born days.

7   ALICE. Well, you can blame our Billy for that, because I do. I've not finished with that Rita-whatever-her-name-is. I shall find out where she lives. I shall go round and I shall find out.

8   GEOFFREY. I know her. She works in that milk-bar in Sheep-gate. I know her and I know her bloody father as well. You know him. Him that's always racing that whippet on the moor. Him with them tattoos all up his arms. Supposed to work in the market, when he does work. They live in them terrace-houses. Down Mill Lane.

9   ALICE. Well, I shall go round. I shall go round and see her mother.

10 GEOFFREY. You'll go bloody nowhere. You keep away. We've got enough to cope with without getting mixed up with that lot.

11 ALICE. I only wish she could have been spared it. If you can't die in peace, what can you do?

12 GEOFFREY. You don't want to go fretting yourself about that. She heard nothing about it. She was miles away.

13 ALICE. And what do you say she said? Did she know you?

1 GEOFFREY. Well, she did at first. She was all right after you
went down. And she was all right when our Billy came
up with her medicine. She took that all right and kept
it down. She was just ramblin' on—like she does. She
was chuntering on about a tin of salmon going to waste.
Then something about getting her pension book
changed at the post office next week. She never knew,
you see. It was just this last five minutes when she
started to slaver. I was holding her up in bed and she
just slumped forward. I thought she was having a
bloody fit. But no—she just gave a little jerk with her
head—like that. Then she started to slaver. She was just
like a baby, Alice. Just like a baby, slavering and gasping
for breath. She wet my handkerchief through, I know
that. Then she sits straight up—by herself—and says,
'Where's my Jack?' I had to think who she was talking
about. Then I remember she must have meant your
father. Only she always used to call him John, didn't
she?

2 ALICE [*half to herself*]. She hardly ever called him Jack.

3 GEOFFREY. Then she said, 'I love you, Jack'. Oh, and before
she said, 'What are you thinking about?'—she must
have been talking to your father, she couldn't have
been talking to anyone else. But you had to listen
close to, to hear what she was saying. She could hardly
speak. By the time she went she couldn't speak at all.
She was just slavering.

There is a pause.

4 ALICE. You should have called me.

5 GEOFFREY [*suddenly compassionate*]. She wouldn't have known
you. And you wouldn't have liked to have seen her like
that. You couldn't have done anything for her—
nobody could.

6 ALICE. You should have called me, Geoffrey.

7 GEOFFREY. I didn't think it would have done you any good
to see her, that's all. [*Reverting to his normal tones.*] And,

listen! If he thinks he's going to the funeral in them bloody suède shoes, he's got another think coming. There'll be all them Masonics coming—I'm not having him showing me up. He'll get some bloody black ones or stop at home.

2 ALICE. He's got some black ones but he won't wear them.

3 GEOFFREY. Well, make him. And think on and see that he gets a bloody good wash on Tuesday morning. When did he have a bath last?

4 ALICE. Well, there'll be no baths on Tuesday, 'cause I'm not lighting any fires—I shall be too busy. And I still know nothing about the funeral. I wish I'd have seen Mr. Duxbury.

5 GEOFFREY. You only just missed him. If you'd have gone to your Emily's five minutes later you would have seen him. Anyway, they're doing everything. Shadrack and Duxbury's. He says they'll fix the tea for us—the lot.

5 ALICE. And you still haven't told me what Mr. Duxbury said about our Billy—about him getting into bother at work.

7 GEOFFREY. Don't talk to me about our Billy. I'm going to start putting him in the coal cellar when people come. Duxbury comes to the door—I take him straight upstairs. He starts measuring her up so I left him to it. Come down here and walk into the living-room and there's bloody Dopey sat in here. He's let the fire go out. Kettle boiling it's bloody head off. He's sitting with his shoes and socks off and all muck between his toes watching bloody Noddy on television. [*Losing his temper.*] His grandmother bloody dead upstairs and all he can do is watch Noddy.

8 ALICE. I can't understand him. He doesn't seem to have any feeling for anybody.

9 GEOFFREY. I told him. I said to him, 'What are you bloody doing? Do you know Mr. Duxbury's upstairs?' He was out of that chair and through that door like a shot. I watched him out of our bedroom window—putting

his shoes and socks on in the street. I'll bloody swing
for him before I've finished, I will.

2   ALICE. Well, what did Mr. Duxbury say about him?

3   GEOFFREY. He wasn't going to say anything. Not today.
Until I asked him if our Billy had rung up and asked for
his cards, like he said he was. Then the lot came out.
[*He indicates the calendars.*] There's all these calendars he's
supposed to have posted, for one. Then there's his
petty cash—that doesn't add up. Then there's his
postage book. Two pound ten postage money he's had.
And he's supposed to have pinched a brass plate off a
coffin. What does he want to do a bloody trick like
that for?

4   ALICE. You didn't say anything about postage money before
—you just said petty cash.

5   GEOFFREY. I don't know. Don't ask me. The whole bloody
lot's wrong from start to finish. He can't keep his hands
off nothing.

6   ALICE. But what did he say about not taking him to court?

7   GEOFFREY. How many more bloody times? He says if he stays
on—and does his work right, and pays this money back
—and stops giving back-chat every five minutes—he'll
hear no more about it.

8   ALICE. But what about him going to London?

9   GEOFFREY. How the bloody hell can he go to London? He'll
go to Dartmoor if he's not careful. He's to stop on there
until he's paid this money back—and I know I'm not
paying it, if he goes down on his bended knees I'm not
paying it.

10 ALICE. It's a mystery to me why he wanted to take that
money in the first place. He never buys anything—and
if he does go short he knows he's only to come to me.

11 GEOFFREY. You've been too soft with him, that's been the
bloody trouble, all along. Anyway, you know what he's
spent it on, don't you? That bloody engagement ring.
That's where the money's gone. Well, he can get that

back to the shop for a start. And he can get engaged
when he's twenty-one and not before. And he brings
no more bloody lasses round here. And he comes in at
nine o'clock in future—never mind half-past eleven.
There's going to be some changes in this house.

2 ALICE. Yes, and you've said that before and it's made no
difference. He used to get on her nerves.

3 GEOFFREY. Well, she's not got him to put up with any more.
He used to lead her a dog's life. I've seen him—mocking
her. And where is he? He's got no bloody right to be
out.

4 ALICE. I don't know where he's got to.

5 GEOFFREY. He'll know where he's got to when he rolls in
here. He'll go straight out again—through the bloody
window.

6 ALICE. We don't want any more rows tonight, Geoffrey. My
nerves won't stand it. You've had one row today and
you saw what happened. She was all right till you
started on our Billy.

7 GEOFFREY. Don't start bloody blaming me for it. For God's
sake. I told her often enough to go to see that doctor.

8 ALICE. You know very well she wouldn't go.

9 GEOFFREY. It was your bloody job to see that she did. I'm not
on tap twenty-four hours a bloody day. I've got work
to do.

They are building up to an argument.

10 ALICE. And I've got my work to do as well. I did my best. I
tried to make her go. You know why it was. It was
because he was a blackie.

11 GEOFFREY. I don't care if he was sky-blue bloody pink with
yellow dots on. You should have gone with her.

12 ALICE [*almost in tears*]. It was only this afternoon she was sitting
in that chair with a pot of tea. You can say what you
like, she was all right till you started on to our Billy.

13 GEOFFREY. She was never all right. She hadn't been all right
for bloody months.

1 ALICE. It's tomorrow morning I'm thinking about. When I should be taking her up her pot of tea and a Marie Louise biscuit.

2 GEOFFREY. Will you shut up about bloody pots of tea! You won't fetch her back with pots of bloody tea. She'll get no pots of tea where she's gone.

3 ALICE. Well, I like to think she will! [*She rises and crosses towards the kitchen.*]

4 GEOFFREY. Where are you going now?

5 ALICE. I'm going to make myself one.

6 GEOFFREY. Sit you down. I'll see to it.

7 ALICE. No. No. I'm better when I'm doing something. I'd rather be occupied.

ALICE goes into the kitchen and GEOFFREY crosses to join her.

8 GEOFFREY. I'll give you a hand, anyway.

GEOFFREY goes into the kitchen as the lights fade down in the living-room. The lights come up in the garden—both from the porch and the street lamp. We discover BILLY sitting on the garden seat, rather cold and his hands dug deep in his pockets. He lights a cigarette, then rises and crosses to the front door where he listens for a moment through the letter box. Hearing nothing he returns towards the garden seat and sits disconsolately.

BILLY hums to himself and then turns on the seat and takes up a garden cane. He toys with the cane for a moment, attempting to balance it on his fingers. His humming grows louder and he stands and conducts an imaginary orchestra using the cane as a baton. He is humming a military march and he suddenly breaks off as the garden cane becomes, in his imagination, a rifle. He shoulders the cane and marches briskly up and down the garden path.

9 BILLY [*marching*]. Lef', ri', lef', ri', lef'-ri'-lef'! Halt! [*He halts.*] Order arms! [*He brings the cane down to the 'Order' position.*]

He pauses for a moment and the garden cane becomes, in his imagination, an officer's baton which he tucks under his arm and then he marches smartly off to an imaginary saluting base a few paces away. He has become, in his imagination, a major-general.

Dearly beloved Officers and Gentlemen of the Desert Shock Troops. We are assembled at the grave-side here this evening to pay our respects to a great lady. There are many of us here tonight who would not be alive now but for her tender mercies although in her later years she was limbless from the waist down. She struggled valiantly to combat ignorance and disease. Although she will be remembered by the world as the inventor of penicillin and radium we, of this proud regiment, will remember her as our friend—the Lady of the Lamp. I call upon you all to join with me in observing two minutes' silence.

BILLY *removes an imaginary hat which he places under his arm. He lowers his head respectfully and stands in silence. Imitating a bugle he hums the 'Last Post'. He is still standing, his head lowered, as* ARTHUR *and* LIZ *enter the garden. Although* LIZ *is about the same age as* BARBARA *and* RITA *she has more maturity and self-possession. Although she is dressed casually and is, in fact, wearing the black skirt we have heard so much about, she is not as scruffy as we have been led to believe. She is also wearing a white blouse and a green suède jacket. She is not particularly pretty but is obviously a girl of strong personality.* LIZ *is the only girl for whom* BILLY *has any real feelings.* LIZ *and* ARTHUR *stand for a moment looking at* BILLY, *who has not noticed them.*

2 ARTHUR. What's up with him, then?

3 BILLY [*startled and embarrassed*]. I didn't hear you coming . . . [*He sees* LIZ *for the first time and is even more embarrassed.*] Liz.

4 LIZ. Hallo, Billy.

5 ARTHUR. What are you on, then? He's saying his prayers.

6 BILLY [*he scratches the ground with the cane with an assumed casualness*]. No, I was just standing. Just thinking to myself. [*To* LIZ.] Arthur told me you were back.

7 ARTHUR. You look like one of them stinking gnomes we've got in our garden. With a maring fishing rod. [BILLY *tosses the garden cane into the garden.*] What are you standing out here for? Won't they let you in?

1   BILLY [*irritated*]. Can't I stand in my own rotten garden now?
    [*To* LIZ.] When did you get back?

2   LIZ. Last week.

3   ARTHUR [*before she can continue*]. Hey, is it right your grandma's
    snuffed it?

4   BILLY. You what? Yes. This afternoon. Funeral's on Tuesday.

5   ARTHUR. Fizzing hell! I was only talking to her this morning.

6   BILLY [*to* LIZ]. Why didn't you ring up?

7   ARTHUR [*before she can reply*]. You don't half drop me in it! I
    thought you'd made it up. I told our old lady you'd
    made it up! She'll go stinking bald.

8   BILLY [*to* LIZ.] You've got the number. You could have rung
    me up.

9   LIZ. I was going to, Billy.

10 ARTHUR [*again before she can continue*]. Do you know what I was
    going to do? If I'd had enough money. I was going to
    send a wreath round. With a little card saying in capital
    letters: 'You Stinking Louse-bound Crowing Liar'. I was
    sure you'd made it up.

11 BILLY [*annoyed*]. What are you talking about? What would I
    want to make up a thing like that for?

12 ARTHUR. Oh, get George Washington. [*In a mimicking falsetto.*]
    Please sir, I cannot tell a lie. I chopped up Grandma.

13 BILLY [*turning to* ARTHUR]. Look, why don't you just jack it in—
    eh?

14 ARTHUR. All right, all right. Keep your shirt on. Don't go
    biting my head off.

15 BILLY. Well, you want to grow up.

16 ARTHUR. You what! Listen who's talking. You're a right one
    to talk. Grow up? Blimey! [*He turns to* LIZ.] Do you know
    what he once did? He saves up these plastic boats you
    get out of cornflake packets. He does! He saves them all.
    He keeps them in his desk. Well, do you know what he
    once did? He filled up a baby's coffin with water—
    down in the basement—and started playing at naval
    battles. He thinks I don't know.

1   BILLY. Aw, shut up. Anyway, I don't sit in the lavatory all
    morning. Reading mucky books.

2   ARTHUR. No, and I don't go around playing at Winston
    Churchills when I think nobody's looking.

3   BILLY. Aw, belt up, man!

4   ARTHUR [tapping BILLY on the chest]. You just want to stop telling
    people to belt up. You want to go careful, man. Or else
    somebody's going to belt you.

5   BILLY. Yeh—you and whose army?

6   ARTHUR. I'm not talking about me. I'm talking about some-
    body else.

7   BILLY. Who?

8   ARTHUR. Somebody's brother.

9   BILLY. Whose naffing brother? What are you talking about?

10 ARTHUR. Rita's naffing brother. Who do you think? That's
    what I came up to tell you—thanks very much for ask-
    ing. It's the last favour I'll do you, I know that. I've just
    seen him down at the dance hall. Screaming blue
    murder. I wouldn't like to be in your shoes, man, when
    he gets you.

11 BILLY [uneasily]. I'm not frightened of him.

12 ARTHUR. You what! He'll bloody slaughter you. He will, you
    know, he's not kidding.

13 BILLY. So what.

14 ARTHUR. So what, he says. I knew you should never have
    given her that ring in the first place. I told you, didn't I?
    Well, she still wants it back, you know. You've had your
    chips.

15 BILLY. Aaahh—who cares.

16 ARTHUR. You'll bloody care when you're in the infirmary
    getting stitched up. Well, you've had it coming, matey,
    let's face it. You and your rotten lying. Well, I know
    what I'd do if I was you—and I didn't want to get
    crippled. I'd get off to that job in London, dead smartish
    —that's if there is a job in London.

1   BILLY. What do you mean—if there is a job in London?

2   ARTHUR. I mean, if it isn't another of your stinking lies!

3   BILLY. I'll go—don't you worry.

4   ARTHUR. I'm not worrying, Tosh. I've got more to do with my time. But I'll tell you this much, you can stop going round giving out the patter about our old lady. Because if I hear—once more—about her being in the family way, I'll be round here myself. Never mind Rita's brother.

5   BILLY. Aw—dry up.

6   ARTHUR [*going off*]. Well, I've told you, man. [*He turns to* BILLY.] And don't think I'm covering up for you any more— 'cause I'm not.

7   BILLY [*softly*]. Aw—get knotted.

     ARTHUR *goes.* BILLY *turns to* LIZ.

     He talks too much. [*There is a slight pause as they stand and look at each other.*] . . . Hallo, Liz.

8   LIZ. Hallo, Billy.

9   BILLY. When did you get back?

10   LIZ. Last week.

11   BILLY. Why didn't you ring me up?

12   LIZ. I was going to.

13   BILLY. Thank you very much.

14   LIZ. No—really. I was going to. I thought I'd see you at the dance tonight. I went to the dance. I thought you'd be there.

15   BILLY. I couldn't go.

16   LIZ. No. No—I know. I heard about your grandma. I'm sorry.

17   BILLY. Yes. [*Changing the subject.*] I haven't seen you for months.

18   LIZ. Five weeks. You didn't waste much time, did you?

1 BILLY. Why? What do you mean?

2 LIZ. Getting engaged. To everybody.

3 BILLY. Oh—that.

4 LIZ. You're mad.

5 BILLY [*he shrugs his shoulders*]. Where have you been?

6 LIZ. Oh—here and there.

7 BILLY. Why didn't you write?

8 LIZ. I did—once. I tore it up.

9 BILLY. You're always tearing it up.

10 LIZ [*changing the subject*]. How's everything with you? How's the script-writing? How's the book coming along?

11 BILLY [*enthusiastically*]. Oh, I've finished it. It's going to be published next Christmas. [*She gives him a long, steady look.*] I haven't started writing it yet.

12 LIZ. You are mad.

13 BILLY. Yes. [LIZ *sits on the garden seat.*] Liz?

14 LIZ. Mmmm?

15 BILLY [*sitting beside her*]. Do you find life complicated?

16 LIZ. Mmmm. So-so.

17 BILLY. I wish it was something you could tear up and start again. Life, I mean. You know—like starting a new page in an exercise book.

18 LIZ. Well, it's been done. Turning over a new leaf.

19 BILLY. I turn over a new leaf every day—but the blots show through.

20 LIZ. What's all this about London?

21 BILLY. I've been offered a job down there.

22 LIZ. Honestly?

23 BILLY. Honestly. A sort of job.

24 LIZ. Good. I'm glad. Perhaps it's your new leaf.

25 BILLY [*proud of the phrase*]. I turn over a new leaf every day—but the blots show through the page.

1　LIZ. Well, perhaps a new leaf isn't good enough. Perhaps you need to turn over a new volume.

2　BILLY. Yes.

3　LIZ. Are you going to take that job?

4　BILLY. I think so.

5　LIZ. You only think so?

6　BILLY. I don't know.

7　LIZ. You know, my lad, the trouble with you is that you're —what's the word?—introspective. You're like a child at the edge of a paddling pool. You want very much to go in, but you think so much about whether the water's cold, and whether you'll drown, and what your mother will say if you get your feet wet....

8　BILLY [*interrupting*]. All I'm doing is wondering whether to dive or swim.

9　LIZ. Perhaps you need a coach.

10　BILLY. Do you know why I'm so fascinated by London?

11　LIZ. No. Why?

12　BILLY. A man can lose himself in London. London is a big place. It has big streets—and big people.

13　LIZ [*giving him another look*]. Mad.

14　BILLY. Perhaps I need to turn over a new paddling pool.

　　　There is a pause as they look at each other.

15　LIZ. Who do you love?

16　BILLY [*adopting his thick north country accent*]. Thee, lass.

17　LIZ. Yes, it sounds like it, doesn't it?

18　BILLY. I do, lass.

19　LIZ. Say it properly, then.

20　BILLY. I do, Liz. I do.

21　LIZ. What about Barbara?

22　BILLY. Well, what about her?

23　LIZ. Well, *what* about her?

24　BILLY. All over.

1   LIZ. You've said that before.

2   BILLY. I know. This time it is all over.

3   LIZ. And what about the other one? Rita-whatever-her-
    name-is?

4   BILLY. That's all over, too.

There is a pause. BILLY *takes out a packet of cigarettes, lights two
and gives one to* LIZ.

5   LIZ. I want to marry you, you know, Billy.

6   BILLY. I know, Liz—I know. We will—one day.

7   LIZ. Not one day. Now.

8   BILLY. Do you?

9   LIZ. Next week will do. Before you go to London. Or when
    you get there. Whichever you prefer.

10 BILLY. I think I get engaged a bit too often.

11 LIZ. I don't want to get engaged. I want to get married.

12 BILLY. Is that why you keep sloping off every few weeks?
    Because you want to get married?

13 LIZ. I want to get married.

14 BILLY. All right. All right.

15 LIZ. How do you mean—all right? I've just proposed to you
    and you say 'all right'. Aren't you supposed to say 'this
    is so sudden' or 'yes' or something.

16 BILLY. I don't know.

LIZ *puts her arms round him and kisses him. He responds. They break
away.*

17 LIZ. Billy?

18 BILLY. Yes?

19 LIZ. You know what you wanted me to do? That night?
    When we walked through the park? And I said 'another
    night'?

20 BILLY. I remember.

21 LIZ. Well, it's another night tonight, isn't it?

73

1   BILLY [*afraid but excited*]. Are you sure?

2   LIZ. Yes.

3   BILLY. Where could we go?

4   LIZ. I've got a room. There's no one there.

5   BILLY. What do you think we ought to do about—you know, babies.

6   LIZ. Have them. Lots and lots of them.

7   BILLY. No, I mean tonight.

8   LIZ. It's all right. [*After a pause.*] Billy?

9   BILLY. Yes?

10   LIZ. Ask you something?

11   BILLY. What?

12   LIZ. Do you know what *virgo intacta* means?

13   BILLY. Yes.

14   LIZ. Well, I'm not.

15   BILLY. No. I somehow didn't think you were.

16   LIZ. Want me to tell you about it?

17   BILLY. No. [*He kisses her.*] All right, yes. Tell me about it.

18   LIZ. No—not now.

19   BILLY. Tell me about it.

20   LIZ. You think that's why I'm always going away, don't you?

21   BILLY. I don't know.

22   LIZ. Ask me where I've been for the past five weeks.

23   BILLY. What difference does it make?

24   LIZ. None—I suppose. It's just that every so often I want to go away. It's not you, Billy. I want to be here with you. It's the town. It's the people we know. I don't like knowing everybody—or becoming a part of things. Do you see what I mean?

25   BILLY. Yes . . . yes.

26   LIZ. What I'd like is to be invisible. You know, to be able to move around without people knowing, and not having

to worry about them. Not having to explain all the time.

2 BILLY. Liz . . . Liz! Listen! Listen! Liz, do you know what I do?
When I want to feel invisible. I've never told anybody.
I have a sort of—well, it's an imaginary country. Where
I go. It has its own people. . . .

3 LIZ [*interrupting*]. Do you do that? I knew you would. Why are
we so alike, Billy? I can read your thoughts. A town like
this. Only somewhere over by the sea. And we used to
spend the whole day on the beach. That's what I used
to think about.

4 BILLY. This is more than a town—it's a whole country. [*He
is getting excited.*] I'm supposed to be the Prime Minister.
You're supposed to be the Foreign Secretary—or
something.

5 LIZ [*with mock obedience*]. Yes, sir.

6 BILLY. I think about it for hours. Sometimes I think, if we
were married, with a house of our own, we could just
sit and imagine ourselves there.

7 LIZ. Yes, we could.

8 BILLY. I want a room, in the house, with a green baize door.
It will be a big room, and when we go into it, through
the door, that's it, that's our country. No one else would
be allowed in. No one else will have keys. They won't
know where the room is. Only we'll know. And we'll
make models of the principal cities. You know, out of
cardboard. And we could use toy soldiers. Painted. For
the people. We could draw maps. It would be a place to
go to on a rainy afternoon. We could go there. No one
would find us. I thought we could have a big sloping
shelf running all the way down one wall, you know,
like a big desk. And we'd have a lot of blank paper on
it and design our own newspapers. We could even make
uniforms, if we wanted to. It would be our country . . .
[*He falters away.*]

9 LIZ. Let's have a model train that the kids won't be allowed
to use.

10 BILLY. Liz . . .? Will you marry me?

1 LIZ. Yes. [*He kisses her.*] Billy?

2 BILLY. Yes?

3 LIZ. Are you really going to London or just pretending?

4 BILLY. I'm thinking about it.

5 LIZ. Only thinking?

6 BILLY. Well, going. Soon, anyway.

7 LIZ. When's soon?

8 BILLY. Well, soon.

9 LIZ. That's a bit vague. Soon. Why not now?

10 BILLY. It's difficult.

11 LIZ. No, it's easy. You just get on a train and four hours later there you are—in London.

12 BILLY. It's easy for you, you've had the practice.

13 LIZ. I'll come with you.

14 BILLY. That'd be marvellous—if we could.

15 LIZ [*she rises*]. But we can, Billy! We can! What is there to stop us?

16 BILLY [*thinking seriously about it for the first time*]. Well, there's . . . I don't know . . . you've got to make all sorts of arrangements, haven't you?

17 LIZ. You buy a ticket, that's all. You buy a ticket and get on a train. That's all there is to it.

18 BILLY. I've never thought about it like that.

19 LIZ. Billy, we can! We can go! We can go tonight!

20 BILLY. But, Liz.

21 LIZ. There's the midnight train. We can catch that. It gets in at King's Cross Station. Breakfast at Lyons Corner House. Then we get a tube—we get a tube from Piccadilly Circus to Earl's Court. I've got friends there, Billy. They'll put us up. They'd give us a room.

22 BILLY [*almost convinced. He rises*]. Tonight, Liz?

1 LIZ. Yes, tonight! Twelve-five from New Street Station. We'll be in London tomorrow. We can go to Hyde Park in the afternoon. We'll go to the pictures tomorrow night—the Odeon. Marble Arch, What time is it now?

2 BILLY [*glancing at his watch*]. Just after ten.

3 LIZ. I'm going, Billy. Are you coming?

4 BILLY [*his mind made up*]. Yes, Liz. I'm coming.

5 LIZ. Are you sure?

6 BILLY. I'm coming with you.

7 LIZ [*briskly*]. Right, then. I'm going home. Now. And I'm going to pack my things. I'll meet you at the station. In that refreshment room. In an hour's time. Eleven o'clock. I'll get the tickets. Two singles to London. You won't let me down, Billy?

8 BILLY. I'm coming.

9 LIZ. What will you tell your father and mother?

10 BILLY. They know already—more or less.

11 LIZ. You won't let them talk you out of it?

12 BILLY. I'm coming.

The lights begin to come up in the living-room. GEOFFREY *enters from the kitchen, takes up a newspaper, sits down and begins to read. The lights fade slightly in the garden.*

13 LIZ [*she kisses* BILLY]. Eleven o'clock.

14 BILLY. Eleven.

LIZ *goes off down the garden.* BILLY *watches her go and then turns and enters the house.* GEOFFREY *rises at the sound of the door.* BILLY *enters the living-room. He registers shock as he sees that his cupboard has been opened.*

15 GEOFFREY. What time of bloody night do you call this?

16 BILLY. It's only ten.

17 GEOFFREY. I don't care what bloody time it is. Who said you could go out? And where've you been?

1 BILLY. I've only been out. Why? Did you want some chips bringing in?

2 GEOFFREY. I'll chip you. I'll chip you round your bloody ear-hole if I start on you. Have you been out dancing?

3 BILLY. No, 'course I haven't.

4 GEOFFREY. If you've been out dancing with your grandma lying dead I'll bloody murder you, I will.

5 BILLY [*feigning innocence*]. What's up?

6 GEOFFREY. What's up—you know what's up. What have you done with that letter of your mother's?

BILLY *glances in fear at the envelopes on the floor.*

Do you hear me? I'm talking to you!

7 BILLY. What letter?

8 GEOFFREY. What, what, what! Don't keep saying bloody 'what'. You know what letter. That what she gave you to post to 'Housewives' Choice'.

9 BILLY. I told her once. I posted it.

10 GEOFFREY [*taking the letter from his pocket*]. You posted bloody nothing. You've had it in that cupboard. It was given to you to post. You bloody idle little swine.

11 BILLY. I did post it. That's just the rough copy.

12 GEOFFREY. What are you talking about? Rough copy? It's your mother's letter. How could you have posted it?

13 BILLY. Look—the letter my mother wrote was full of mistakes, that's all. I just thought it would stand a better chance if I wrote it out again—properly. That's all.

ALICE *enters from the kitchen.*

14 GEOFFREY. Well, who told you to write it out again? And who told you to open it? You keep your thieving hands off other people's things! And where did you get all them bloody calendars from, as well?

15 BILLY. What calendars?

1 GEOFFREY [*fingering his belt*]. By bloody hell! I'll give you 'what' if you don't stop saying 'what, what', my lad! You know what! Don't think I haven't been talking to Mr. Duxbury—because I have. I've heard it all. You make me a laughing-stock. You can't keep you hands off nothing. And where's that monkey wrench out of my garage? I suppose you know nothing about that?

2 BILLY. No, 'course I don't. What do I want with a monkey wrench?

3 GEOFFREY. What do you want with two hundred bloody calendars! And what have you been doing with their name-plates as well? You're not right in the bloody head.

4 BILLY [*losing his temper*]. I'm not right! I'm not right! I didn't want to work for Shadrack and flaming Duxbury's! You made me take the rotten job! Now you can answer for it.

5 GEOFFREY. Don't bloody shout at me, you gormless young get—or I'll knock your eyes out.

6 BILLY. God give me strength.

7 GEOFFREY. Give you strength, he wants to give you some sense! You're like a bloody Mary-Ann! Well, I hope your mother gets more sense out of you.

8 ALICE. Well, you've got yourself into a fine mess, lad, haven't you?

9 BILLY. Have I?

10 ALICE. I'm only thankful she knows nothing about it. [*She glances up at the ceiling.*] Why didn't you post that letter of mine?

11 BILLY. I did post it. I was telling Dad. I just wrote it out again, that's all. There was some mistakes in it.

12 ALICE. Yes, well we can't all be Shakespeares, can we? And what's all this about you taking money from work?

13 BILLY. What money?

14 GEOFFREY [*warningly*]. I've told you.

15 BILLY. What? I haven't taken any money.

1   GEOFFREY. There's two pound ten short in your postage book. Never mind petty cash.

2   BILLY. Oh, that . . . I. . . .

3   ALICE. What did you do with it, Billy?

4   GEOFFREY. He's spent it. That's what he's bloody done with it.

5   ALICE. Well, it's just beyond me. You didn't have to take money, Billy. You could have come to me.

6   GEOFFREY. You've had things too bloody easy. That's been your trouble. You can't carry on at work like you do at home, you know.

7   BILLY. Well, I told you I didn't want to work there when I first started, didn't I?

8   GEOFFREY. You didn't want to work for nobody, if you ask me anything. You thought you'd live on me, didn't you?

9   BILLY. No, I didn't. I could have kept myself.

10 ALICE. Kept yourself—how?

11 BILLY. Writing scripts.

12 GEOFFREY. Writing bloody scripts, you want to get a day's work done, never mind writing scripts. Who do you think's going to run this bloody business when I'm gone?

13 BILLY. You said you didn't want me in the business.

14 GEOFFREY. Only because you were so bloody idle! Somebody's got to carry on with it! Who's going to keep your mother?

15 BILLY [with an attempt at humour]. Why, you're not retiring, are you?

16 GEOFFREY. Don't try and be funny with me, lad! Or you'll laugh on the other side of your face!

17 ALICE. And what did you tell me about Arthur's mother? She wasn't having a baby, you know very well she wasn't.

18 BILLY. It was only a joke.

1   GEOFFREY. A joke—it sounds like a bloody joke!

2   ALICE. And why did you tell her I'd broken my leg?

3   BILLY. I didn't know you knew Arthur's mother.

4   ALICE. Yes, you don't know who I know and who I don't
    know, do you? If you want to know, she rang me up.
    And what did you do with that cardigan she gave you
    for me, last Christmas?

5   BILLY [*vaguely*]. I think I gave it to the refugees.

6   ALICE. Well, you've got a new cardigan to find by tomorrow
    morning. Because she's coming round to see me.

7   BILLY [*emphatically*]. I won't be here tomorrow morning.

8   GEOFFREY. You won't be here to bloody night if you talk to
    your mother in that tone of voice!

9   BILLY. I'm not going to be here tonight. I'm leaving.

10 ALICE. What are you talking about?

11 BILLY [*decisively*]. I'm getting the midnight train. Tonight. I'm
    taking that job in London.

12 ALICE. If you're in any more trouble, Billy, it's not some-
    thing you can leave behind you. You put it in your
    suitcase and take it with you.

13 GEOFFREY. Well, he's not taking that suitcase of mine up-
    stairs. [*Turning to* BILLY.] Anyway, you're not going to
    London or nowhere else—so you can get that idea out
    of your head, for a kick-off.

14 BILLY. I mean it, Dad. I'm going.

15 GEOFFREY. And I bloody mean it, as well. [*Raising his voice.*]
    You stop here till that money's paid back. You can
    thank your lucky stars Mr. Duxbury's not landed you
    in court. You want to be grateful.

16 BILLY. Grateful! Grateful! Grateful for this, grateful for that!
    That's all I've heard ever! Grateful you let me go to the
    grammar school! We've been hearing that one since
    the first day I went there. What am I supposed to do?
    Say 'thank you very much' three times a day for my
    marvellous education?

1   GEOFFREY. Well, it's a chance we never had!

2   BILLY. Yes, and don't we bloody well know it! I even had to be grateful for winning my own scholarship! And what did you say when I came running home to tell you I'd won it? Don't think I've forgotten! I was eleven years old! I came belting out of those school gates and I ran all the way! Just to tell you! And what did you say? That you'd have to pay for the uniform and I'd have to be grateful! And now I'm supposed to be grateful to Shadrack and stinking Duxbury! Why? What for? For letting me sit at one of their rotten desks all day?

3   ALICE [*gently reasoning*]. Well, you took the job, Billy.

4   GEOFFREY. Yes, and he's stopping there till that money's paid back.

5   BILLY. I'm not arguing about it. I'm going! [*He crosses towards the door.*]

6   GEOFFREY. Go, then! I've finished with you!

> BILLY *enters the hall and moves up the stairs.* GEOFFREY *crosses to the door and calls after* BILLY *as he goes into the bedroom.*

> They'll take you to court, you know! I won't stop them! I'm not paying it back! And don't think you're taking my suitcase!

> GEOFFREY *crosses back into the living-room and stands silent.* ALICE *sits in the chair by the fire.*

7   ALICE. Oh, dear me . . . Oh, dear me.

> BILLY *enters from the bedroom and charges down the stairs and into the living-room. He is carrying a small battered suitcase. He crosses to the sideboard and, opening a drawer, begins to pack the case with shirts, socks, ties and a pullover.* GEOFFREY *watches him in silence.*

8   ALICE [*concerned*]. What time train do you reckon you're catching?

9   BILLY. Midnight.

10   ALICE Well, what time does it get in?

1 BILLY. Tomorrow morning.

2 ALICE. And where are you going to live when you get there?

3 GEOFFREY. He'll finish up in the Salvation Army Hostel.

4 ALICE [*as* BILLY *packs a pair of socks*]. All them socks need darning, you know. [BILLY *makes no reply.*] Well, you'll want more than one suit . . . And what about your grandma's funeral on Tuesday?

   BILLY *has now placed all his clothing in the case. He stoops and begins to pack the calendars.*

5 GEOFFREY [*in disbelief*]. What the thump are you packing them bloody calendars for?

6 BILLY. I thought I'd post them.

7 ALICE. Well, you'll be expected at the funeral, you know.

8 GEOFFREY [*disparagingly*]. He's not going anywhere.

9 BILLY [*slamming the case shut he rises*]. I'm going.

   He picks up the case and crosses to the door.

10 GEOFFREY [*half-relenting*]. Don't act so bloody daft.

   BILLY *pauses for a moment, his hand on the door, caught up in the embarrassment of leaving.*

11 BILLY. Well, I'll write to you then. Soon as I've got fixed up. [*Acutely embarrassed.*] I'm sorry about my grandma.

   He goes out.

12 ALICE. Oh, dear me . . . Oh, dear me.

13 GEOFFREY. They can summons him. I've finished.

14 ALICE. You'll have to pay it, Geoffrey. Will he be all right on his own?

15 GEOFFREY. He won't bloody go—he'll be back in five minutes.

16 ALICE. We know nothing about where he's going and what he's supposed to be doing. Who's that fellow he says he's going to work for? That comedian?

17 GEOFFREY. I don't bloody know.

1 ALICE. It was in that letter he had in his pocket in that old raincoat.

> GEOFFREY *crosses and takes the envelope from the raincoat which is hanging in the hall. He returns into the living-room reading the letter to himself as he walks. He then reads the letter aloud to* ALICE.

2 GEOFFREY. 'Dear Mr. Fisher, Many thanks for script and gags, I can use some of the gags and pay accordingly. As for my staff job, well I regret to tell you, I do not have staff beside my agent, but several of the boys do work for me, you might be interested in this. [*He pauses.*] Why not call in for a chat next time you are in London? Best of luck and keep writing. Danny Boon.'

3 ALICE [*after pause*]. Run down to the station and fetch him back.

4 GEOFFREY. He's off his bloody rocker.

5 ALICE. You'll have to stop him, Geoffrey.

6 GEOFFREY. Nay, he's big enough to look after himself now. He can stand on his own two feet for a change. I've finished. I've done my whack for him.

7 ALICE. I wonder if he's got any money?

8 GEOFFREY. That's his look-out. It doesn't belong to him if he has. You can depend on that.

9 ALICE. Oh, dear me . . . Oh, dear me.

10 GEOFFREY. There's no need for him to starve. He can get a job if he sets his mind to it. And get up in a morning.

11 ALICE. Well, what's he going to do?

12 GEOFFREY. He can go clerking—same as here. There's a lot of offices in London. Well, there's one thing certain. I know what I'm going to bloody do: I'm off to bed. I've enough on my plate without worrying my head over that one. He can go to hell, he can.

13 ALICE. Do you want a cup of Ovaltine, or anything?

14 GEOFFREY. No. You want to get off to bed as well, lass.

15 ALICE [*rising*]. I always used to take her one up at this time. I'll have to get used to it—not having to.

1   GEOFFREY. Aye, well . . .

2   ALICE. Is the back door locked, Geoffrey?

3   GEOFFREY. I've seen to it.

They cross into the hall. GEOFFREY *switches off the light in the living-room and automatically drops the catch on the Yale lock.* GEOFFREY *follows* ALICE *up the stairs. As they go up, the porch light fades up and* RITA *and* ARTHUR *enter the garden.*

[*With assumed cheerfulness.*] Well, he'll come home at holiday times. And happen some week-ends.

GEOFFREY *switches out the hall light from the top of the stairs and follows* ALICE *into the bedroom.*

4   ARTHUR [*with relief as he sees the hall light go out*]. They've gone to bed.

5   RITA. Have a look through the rotten letter-box.

6   ARTHUR. You can see! They've gone to bed. You don't think they're sitting there with no lights on, do you?

7   RITA. Well, he's not getting out of it—'cause I shall come round in the morning. Our kid'll come round as well. Our kid'll duff him up. He'll get that ring back.

8   ARTHUR. You and your kid and the louse-bound ring! Come on, let's get down to Foley Bottoms. Get some snogging hours in.

9   RITA. He needn't think he's got away with it—'cause he hasn't. He'll be a stretcher case tomorrow morning. [*She screams up at the bedrooms.*] You'll be a stretcher case tomorrow morning! You wait! You rotten yellow-bellied squint-eyed get! You're nothing else! You closet!

We hear the sound of a window being flung open and ALICE *shouting.*

10   ALICE. Get away! Don't you know we've got somebody dead in this house!

We hear the window slammed shut.

1 RITA [*screaming*]. You want to be all rotten dead! You want gassing!

2 ARTHUR. Shut up, Rita! She knows my mother.

3 RITA. I don't care.

4 ARTHUR. They're not worth bothering about. Come on— let's get down to Foley Bottoms. We're just wasting time stuck here.

RITA *allows* ARTHUR *to place his arm around her and pilot her out of the garden.*

5 RITA. Well, we'll be round here first thing tomorrow morn-ing. [*As they go.*] We get up before they do.

ARTHUR *and* RITA *go off. There is a pause and then* BILLY *enters and walks slowly and dejectedly to the front door. He puts down his case and, taking a key from his pocket, opens the door and enters. He crosses into the living-room and, closing the door behind him, switches on the light. He stands indecisively for a moment and then crosses and switches on the radio. He crosses to his suitcase and opens it as the sound of a dance-band comes from the radio. He stands for a moment and, as the music continues, he compulsively lifts his hand and begins to conduct. He glances towards the ceiling, wondering if he is making too much noise, then crosses and switches off the radio. He returns to the suitcase which he carries over to the sideboard. He opens his cupboard and is neatly stacking the calendars back into the cupboard, as*

THE CURTAIN FALLS

The Play in Production

and Questions for Discussion

(H 970)

Billy Liar started life as a novel. The play is, however, more than a mechanical 'adaptation'. A film made soon after the play added yet a third version. It is interesting to compare these various versions: the differences of emphasis help our understanding of the characters and ideas. (The novel was the work of Keith Waterhouse on his own: for the play and the film he was joined as co-author by Willis Hall, an already experienced playwright.)

The most obvious differences result quite simply from the problems of stage-setting. The book takes us round the town of Stradhoughton, its cafés, dance-hall, 'stinking urinal', cemetery, the undertakers' office, the rubbish tip, and much that is in the novel could not be shown on the stage. (Although, as Robert Muller suggests in his review on *page 103*, it would have been possible to have constructed a multi-scene play that involved more of the characters from the novel and showed more of the locales.) What we lose most in this way is the withering attacks in Billy's descriptions of the dreary but pretentious small provincial towns:

> 'The very name of Stradhoughton,' Man o' the Dales had written in the *Stradhoughton Echo* one morning when there was nothing much doing, 'conjures up sturdy buildings of honest native stone, gleaming cobbled streets, and that brackish air which gives this corner of Yorkshire its own especial *piquancy*.' Man o' the Dales put piquancy in italics, not me.
>
> My No. 1 thinking often featured long sessions with Man o' the Dales in whatever pub the boys on the *Echo* used, and there I would put him right on his facts. The cobbled streets, gleaming or otherwise, had long ago been ripped up with the tramlines and re-lined with concrete slabs or tarmacadam— gleaming tarmacadam I would *grant* him, stabbing him in the chest with the stocky briar which in this particular role I affected. The brackish air I was no authority on, except to say that when the wind was in a certain direction it smelled of burning paint. As for the honest native stone, our main street, Moorgate, was— despite the lying reminiscences of old men like Councillor Duxbury who remembered sheep-troughs where the X-L Disc Bar now stands—exactly like any other High Street in Great Britain. Woolworth's looked like Woolworth's, the Odeon looked like the Odeon, and the *Stradhoughton Echo*'s own office, which

> Man o' the Dales must have seen, looked like a public lavatory in honest native white tile. I had a fairly passionate set piece all worked out on the subject of rugged Yorkshire towns, with their rugged neon signs and their rugged plate-glass and plastic shop-fronts, but so far nobody had given me the opportunity to start up on the theme. *(page 17, Longmans edition)*

The squalid dullness of the town is one of the forces that drives Billy into his fantasy world. It is present far more vividly in the novel than it can be in the play. In his descriptions of Stradhoughton Billy reveals to us his apartness so that we are more likely to sympathize with his frustrated and drifting ambitions. He sees, in a way that no one else in the book does, how limited the life of the town is:

> The Roxy was the last splash of light before Stradhoughton petered out and the moors took over. It was supposed to be a suburban amenity or something; at any rate its red, humming neon sign spluttered out the words 'Come Dancing' six nights a week, and all the grown-up daughters of the cold new houses round about converged on it in their satin frocks, carrying their dance shoes in paper bags advertising pork pies. Youths who had come from all over Stradhoughton for the catch sat around on the low brick banisters by the entrance, combing their hair and jeering at each other. *(page 103)*

Billy's employers, Shadrack and Duxbury, are not shown on the stage. The only impression we get of his work with them is his outburst against their 'rotten desks'. The novelist, on the other hand, is able to picture for us Shadrack 'with his little notebook and the propelling pencil rattling against his teeth', and his 'nasal, nosy voice', and Councillor Duxbury:

> He crossed the floor to his own office with an old man's shuffle, putting all his thought into the grip of his stick and the pattern of the faded, broken lino. A thick, good coat sat heavily on his bowed back, and there were enamelled medallions on his watch-chain. At the door of his room he half-turned, moving his whole body like an old robot, and muttered: 'Morning, lads.' *(page 23)*

Billy detests the falsity of both Shadrack's commercialized Christmas calendars and Duxbury's artificially preserved Yorkshire accent. The two symbolize the emptiness of the town, in which chromium-plate, plastic, and plate-glass thinly cover a sordid and cliché-ridden life. Billy, we are made to feel by the novelist, is a conscious liar in a town of lies that includes the false glamour of Miss Stradhoughton 'with her cardboard crown and her satin sash, smiling toothily' and the false romance of the Witch, 'contriving a dazed expression'. Clearly Billy's description of Stradhoughton life is a measure not merely of his restlessness, but also of his imaginative superiority.

Much of this has gone from the play, although it is remarkable what close similarities of detail there are between novel and play. Often sequences of dialogue re-appear word for word. Here, for instance, is Billy's description in the novel of his mother yelling for him to get up:

> I waited until she called: 'If I come up there you'll know about it.'

and a page later, when Billy is still in bed:

> I put the ballpoint away and shoved the envelope back in my pocket, and on the cue of cry number seven, by far my favourite ('Your boiled egg's stone cold and I'm not cooking another') I went downstairs. (page 5)

These two snippets will be found, run together, in Alice's part in the play (page 3, speech 14):

> Billy! Billy! I shan't tell you again. If I come up there you'll know about it! I suppose you know what time it is! Your boiled egg's stone cold and I'm not cooking another.

There are other occasions in the play where dialogue is re-used, but given to a different character. One of these shows how, although very closely linked with the original, the alterations in the play have changed the emphasis considerably. In the novel Florence's final attack is described by Alice as she and Billy wait on the old padded bench in the infirmary corridor:

> There we were all just sitting watching television . . . when she just slumped forward in her chair. We thought she were having a fit, but no, she just gave a little jerk with her head, uh, like that there. . . . Then she started to slaver. She were just like a baby. It was pitiful, pitiful. Just like a baby, slavering and gasping for breath. (page 137)

and later in the description, which is punctuated in the novel by Billy's wandering thoughts, Alice goes on:

> You had to listen close to, to hear what she was saying. She

> could hardly speak, and by the time we got there she couldn't
> speak at all. She was just slavering.

We are made to feel strongly critical of Alice's account by Billy's
comments. He says:

> She spoke hoarsely, in a resigned way. . . . I knew, for I had seen
> her lips moving, that she was already rehearsing the text of this
> eventful day, plucking at the details of it like pomegranate seeds
> and stringing them together in a long rosary that would be
> fingered on and off long after anyone ceased to care.

and later in the account:

> I found it difficult to feel anything beyond indignation that my
> grandmother should be seen off with this gossiping commentary.

After the news of Florence's actual death has been given, Billy
says:

> I could only marvel at the clichés that she used like crutche.
> to take her limping from one crisis to another.

In the play, on the other hand, Florence dies in Geoffrey's
presence, and almost exactly the same words that Alice used are
spoken by Geoffrey when he describes the death to Alice a little
later (*page 62, speeches 1–3*). The effect of these same words in
Geoffrey's mouth is entirely different, particularly as Billy's
critical commentary is not brought to bear on them. We are
made to see Geoffrey in a new light, and realize that behind his
rough 'bloodies' there is some sympathy that rarely manages to
come through. Immediately after giving that same description,
he is made to add a few lines which support our new impression
of Geoffrey, and for which there is no source in the novel:

> GEOFFREY [*suddenly compassionate*]. She wouldn't have known you.
> And you wouldn't have liked to have seen her like that. You
> couldn't have done anything for her—nobody could.
> ALICE. You should have called me, Geoffrey.
> GEOFFREY. I didn't think it would have done you any good to see
> her, that's all.
>
> *(page 62, speeches 5–7)*

However, he immediately reverts to his brusque attacks on
Billy.

There is, in fact, added emphasis on Geoffrey in the play,
which is linked with the decision to limit the action to the
confines of the house, the spirit of which is shown by the

The designer's sketch for the composite set in the 1960 production

description of the furnishings as 'new', 'flashy', and 'in dreadful taste'. The oppressive complacence of suburban life, with its limited horizons, is forced upon us by the permanent set filling the stage. (See the sketch by Alan Tagg for his original set design overleaf.) It could be argued that some of these changes do no more than alter the background against which a part of the action is played. But even the simplest of these changes contributes to this exploration of *family* tension. For instance, in the novel Billy's final ditherings about whether to go to London or not take place at the station with Liz. In the play, we see Billy with his mother and father, and Geoffrey's resigned acceptance is an indication of the limitations of the Fisher family life:

> ALICE. You'll have to stop him, Geoffrey.
> GEOFFREY. Nay, he's big enough to look after himself now. He can stand on his own two feet for a change. I've finished. I've done my whack for him.
>
> *(page 84, speeches 5 and 6)*

Certain of the changes which portray the family background are more important still, and have no equivalent in the novel. Two are essential to the play. The first is the scene after tea with Barbara when Geoffrey talks to his son *(pages 31–33)*. Here we see again that Geoffrey has some sympathy and a clumsy wish to express it. He is trying to communicate with his son, but we realize how hopelessly caught he is in the habits of family life developed over the years. Within minutes Geoffrey and Billy are engaged in the most hideous of their rows.

The second new section which is so important to this emphasis on Geoffrey is one which shows us his limitations. Rita's foulmouthed explosion at the end of Act Three makes a colourful moment, but the real climax of the play has come a little earlier when Geoffrey and Billy have their final confrontation—again one for which there is no source in the novel:

> BILLY. I mean it, Dad. I'm going.
> GEOFFREY. And I bloody mean it, as well. [*Raising his voice.*] You stop here till that money's paid back. You can thank your lucky stars Mr. Duxbury's not landed you in court. You want to be grateful.
> BILLY. Grateful! Grateful! Grateful for this, grateful for that! That's all I've heard ever! Grateful you let me go to the grammar school! We've been hearing that one since the first day I went there. What am I supposed to do? Say 'thank you

very much' three times a day for my marvellous education?
GEOFFREY. Well, it's a chance we never had!
BILLY. Yes, and don't we bloody well know it! I even had to be grateful for winning my own scholarship! And what did you say when I came running home to tell you I'd won it? Don't think I've forgotten! I was eleven years old! I came belting out of those school gates and I ran all the way! Just to tell you! And what did you say? That you'd have to pay for the uniform and I'd have to be grateful! And now I'm supposed to be grateful to Shadrack and stinking Duxbury! Why? What for? For letting me sit at one of their rotten desks all day?

(page 81, speech 14 to page 82, speech 2)

On first thoughts, then, we may regret the necessity for the theatre to do without the satirical descriptions of Stradhoughton. We find, however, that the play brings out a more universal theme as a result of the concentration on the claustrophobic family atmosphere which offers Billy neither stimulation nor sympathetic understanding. This is shown most vividly through the deepened and extended part of Geoffrey. The resulting comedy explores the results of a failure of imagination, of feeling, and above all of communication. Billy may be an oddity that makes us laugh, but his fantasy-ridden world is no more than a perversion of the extra spark of youthful imagination that he has but his parents have long ago lost.

M. M.

A PRODUCTION NOTE BY THE AUTHORS

Taken at its face value, *Billy Liar* could be produced as a simple comedy about a boy who tells lies. There is, however, much more in it than this and the rewarding production will be the one that realizes the strong dramatic theme which lies below the surface. Beneath the comedy runs the story of an imaginative youth fighting to get out of his complacent, cliché-ridden background. The director should not regard Billy as being a freak or a buffoon; the life of fantasy which he lives exists in most people but perhaps Billy's fantasies are nearer to the surface than most. The snatches of fantasy-life which are seen in the play should be directed for reality rather than comedy, and with subtlety rather than with the heavy hand which would take it dangerously near to farce. A production in which Billy is directed purely for laughs in the first two acts will find its audience unprepared to accept the serious content of the third act when Billy, for a time, sheds his final skins of make-believe.

Although Billy is the central character, his importance in the play can be seen only in contrast to his stolid family, and so it is important that his father, his mother and his grandmother should be seen as real persons and not as feeds. Similarly with the three girls it is necessary that Barbara and Rita should not be caricatures but should, in fact, be as real as Liz. On first reading of the text it will be seen that many of the lines are very funny—it must be appreciated however that the same lines are carefully naturalistic. It is this naturalism that the director should aim for in production. It may help the director to read the original novel on which the play was based.

Billy must remember that although he is very different from the rest of his family he is still a member of it. He has the family accent and the family mannerisms. Even when falling into fantasy his accent should not change all that much. For example, in the officer fantasy in Act Three, Billy will find that he will get a better effect by being a northern boy trying to imitate officer-class accents than by being the accomplished actor giving a skilful imitation of an officer. Billy will find that the over-all balance of the play hangs largely upon himself and it will be up to him to carry over the difficult transition of the play from Act Two to Act Three. It is important therefore that Billy's early fantasy scenes are not played as a kind of vaudeville act in an attempt to get as many laughs as possible. Billy must always remember that the purpose of all his fantasy scenes is to give the audience a key to what is going on in his mind.

Geoffrey is a more complex person than the blustering character who appears in Act One. The actor playing Geoffrey might find it helpful to study first the scene in Act Two in which Geoffrey tries to make some contact with Billy; he could then build up the character from this point rather than superimpose this facet of Geoffrey's character on a standard blustering performance. The word 'bloody'—which Geoffrey uses repeatedly—may give some trouble if it is used as an expletive and not as an unconscious punctuation mark in Geoffrey's dialogue. In the case of some amateur societies where the use of the word at all is likely to give offence, the authors give permission for it to be deleted completely—but not for the substitution of euphemisms such as 'ruddy', 'blooming', etc.

Alice is probably the least difficult of the characters to assess. She is a simple uncomplicated woman who has set her values many years ago and never re-examines them, not even in the most extraordinary circumstances. In her evaluation of other people's character she can see no further than the externals— personal appearance, manner of speech, etc. But it will be found that the role of Alice is very important for she is, so to speak, the hub of the circle of people we see in this play. All the arguments revolve around her; nothing takes place in the play that will not affect her in one way or another. Alice, for all her soft-centred self-indulgent outlook is in fact a strong woman and should be cast as such.

Florence is a role which could easily tempt an actress to play a comic cameo without reference to the play at large. Little of Florence's dialogue is sparked off by other characters; she spends most of her time rambling to herself. This is not to say, however, that Florence does not react to what is going on around her. We must feel all the time that she belongs in the family and we should get the impression that she hears a great deal more than she appears to do. We must not get the impression that her day-dreams bear any similarity to Billy's fantasies, for when Florence goes into musings they are confined only to the hard realities of her past.

Barbara, although on one level a stolid, bovine character, is in her own way a fantasist just as much as Billy, for she lives in a woman's magazine world of thatched cottages and tweedy pipe-smoking heroes. Her reaction to Rita arises not too much out of jealousy at a rival as out of revulsion at having to face a side of life not normally on view through her rose-coloured spectacles.

Rita is a difficult character to play in that she has been written deliberately on one note, and a high note at that. The fact is that Rita is a simple, extrovert girl who does not change radically in any given situation. The way in which the actress playing this part should use her skill is in reproducing as accurately as possible the raucous irreverence of this type of working-class girl.

Liz, as can easily be seen, is the character closest to Billy in outlook and temperament. In spite of what we hear about her habits of flitting off from time to time she is not in any way a fey character, but has a down-to-earth quality which she tries to transmit to Billy. Although economically a member of the same class as Billy and his family, she has an outlook transcending its narrow boundaries and lower middle-class traits are not as apparent in her. The most important thing about Liz is that she should radiate warmth and generosity; but in playing her scene with Billy she should remember—as indeed Billy should remember—that this is a scene not about two people in love but two people who are trying to get love from each other.

Arthur is more than a feed for Billy. An ample study of the part will reveal that there is a strong character change in Arthur as the play progresses. He begins in sympathy with Billy and his ideas but, lacking Billy's majestic sweep of vision, he grows jealous and impatient as the play moves along.

The characters in *Billy Liar*—with the exception of working-class Rita—come from a lower middle-class background in an industrial town. They should not have the broad 'Ee bah goom' accents of a mill town, mining town, or other closed northern community, but the simple broad accents of the provinces.

The lighting of the play is very important, especially in the third act. The lighting follows two conventions: the living-room is lit with complete naturalism—standard lamps, overhead light, etc.; but Billy's garden scene in Act Three, where the only natural light is that from the street lamp, gives the producer the opportunity to use his lighting to underline Billy's escape into a world of fantasy. The best effect, when Billy is discovered alone in the garden, is probably to start the scene in the naturalistic evening light of the garden and then, as Billy begins his 'officers and gentlemen' soliloquy, to diminish the lighting gradually until, when we come to the Last Post, Billy is standing in the light of a single spot.

The large set of living-room, hall and garden may pose something of a problem on smaller stages. In such cases it is suggested that the garden scenes be played on the bare stage in front of the living-room, and the garden seat dispensed with. The lighting, of course, should be appropriately changed.

AN ACTOR'S POINT OF VIEW

ALBERT FINNEY, WHO ACTED THE PART OF BILLY IN THE 1960 LONDON PRODUCTION, DESCRIBES HIS FEELINGS ABOUT THE PART.

To me Billy has never been just a comical character. The fact that right at the end of the play he does not go off to London when presented with the opportunity, reveals that he is not equipped to fulfil his dreams, only to indulge in them. This made me feel sorry for him as much as his fantasies made me laugh, and in performing the play the difficulty always was to control the audience enough in the first two acts, so that in the scene with Liz in the third act they were prepared to accept the slightly pathetic elements in him. The first two acts would always get laughs I believe, almost no matter who was performing the play, but if the performers just tried to make the audience laugh as much as possible, they would not have performed this play well and the audience would by this time believe they were present at a farce. Then trying to communicate the other elements in Billy's character in Act Three would be like trying to control a team of six horses that have galloped away with the coach. It is very important in the theatre that the players are always in control of the situation, that they never give the audience its head, particularly in a comedy.

There is a famous theatrical story which will serve as an example of this. The celebrated American husband and wife team of Alfred Lunt and Lynn Fontanne were rehearsing a comedy in the 1930s in New York. The play was in three acts and they felt it got worse in each act; that is that the first act was very funny, the second 'all right', but the third was not funny at all and seemed rather tame. They were such craftsmen of the art of playing comedy that they performed the play so that during the first act they did not allow the audience to laugh although the audience really wanted to. In the second act they allowed them to laugh occasionally, and in the third act they allowed the audience to laugh as much as they wanted, and of course, by this stage in the evening, the audience were absolutely need-ing to laugh. So, by technique, they gave the impression of the play actually improving during the course of the performance. Therefore, you see how important audience control is.

Billy is great fun to act, and everyone is familiar with inventing stories and day-dreaming. Billy, of course, fantasises to an extreme degree, and his dreams are almost more real to him than his everyday life. In acting it, it is terribly important that the actor enjoys the fantasies. Let the spectators laugh, but Billy's attitude to their laughter should be that they do not know what they are missing. In other words, Billy creates any situation he wants to create in his head, but should not laugh at them himself. He should enjoy them and believe them.

I remember myself in my early adolescence playing frogmen in my bed one Sunday morning. At the bottom of the bed was a large tin trunk in which I kept books and sporting equipment, etc., and if I went down the bed headfirst under the clothes, and tapped on the trunk through the bed-clothes, there was a slight-ly muffled metallic sound which I used to pretend was the same effect a frogman would have tapping on the hull of a submarine trapped beneath the surface of the ocean. One morning I was down under the clothes tapping away and talking on the microphone in my frogman's face-mask, as it were, to my colleague on the rescue ship above me, telling him how I was communicating with the men trapped inside the submarine and how many were left alive. Suddenly I felt a tap on my foot which was at the top of the bed. Hastily pulling myself from under the bed-clothes, I saw my father, who had very kindly brought me a cup of tea in bed that morning. As I emerged he said, 'Leave the submarine for a minute and drink your tea or else it'll go cold'. So you can see that Billy's fantasies were very easy for me to understand.

(Photographs of Mr. Finney's performance can be seen between pages 46 and 47.)

REVIEWS OF THE 1960 PRODUCTION

Billy Liar was first produced at the Cambridge Theatre, London, on 13th September, 1960. It was directed by Lindsay Anderson, and the scenery was designed by Alan Tagg. Here is a selection of reactions by some of the critics.

A: THE DRAMATIC CRITIC OF *The Times*

We remember no stage study of a fantast more direct or more complete than we are given in *Billy Liar* at the Cambridge Theatre. Mr. Robert Bolt made a more oblique approach to this type of mind and achieved in *Flowering Cherry* a rather better play; but whatever the shortcomings of the comedy written by Mr. Keith Waterhouse and Mr. Willis Hall, they seem negligible in the light of Mr. Albert Finney's compelling performance of the hero. This actor has no difficulty in persuading us that his part is greater than the play.

He represents a helpless northern country youth who is tugged hither and thither and finally nowhere by an imagination that is like a runaway horse. The most commonplace remark suggests to him a personal fantasy which he at once indulges for the sheer pleasure of the indulgence. He has often to lie to cover his pilferings of petty cash at the office and his lies then have a mad coherence. Just as often he lies when there is nothing to be gained except the joy of inventing something that has never happened or is never likely to happen. He has, for instance, an offer to become a script-writer for a London comedian. Nobody believes him and he does not believe himself in the offer except at moments when the idea presents itself to him as part of the higher truth.

He gets engaged to two girls and spends a great part of the play trying to get the engagement ring he has given to the genteel Barbara back on to the finger of the loud-mouthed Rita who regards it as her property. His ineffectual efforts lead (rather too slowly) to a terrific showdown between the gals. He escapes from them into the arms of Liz who has fantasies of her own and is willing to merge them with his.

After a further showdown with his bullying father and softly sentimental mother he goes away to join Liz on the midnight train to London; but this touch of reality is not to be tolerated by his fantasy-ridden mind and he comes creeping back ignominiously, well knowing that failure and humiliation have no terrors for the obsessed dreamer.

Mr. Finney keeps us continuously interested in both the outer and inner workings of the hero's mind. The farcical confusion into which the industrious and experienced liar finds himself is not less well done than the lighter more delicate pleasures that are known only to the fantast who knows that his invention will never fail him. In a little solo scene of Billy Liar pretending to himself in a night garden Mr. Finney crowns his performance with an extraordinary deft series of imaginings, beginning with the struttings of a drum major and ending with an impressive rendering of Last Post.

Mr. Lindsay Anderson's direction is imaginatively expert, and there are good performances by Miss Mona Washbourne, as the troubled mother, Miss Ethel Griffies, as a maundering old woman whose death startles and seems a little unnecessary, and by Miss Ann Beach, as the genteel little girl who defeats all invitations to a display of passion by chattering domestic trivialities and eating yet another orange.

B: ROBERT MULLER IN THE *Daily Mail*

What emerges here is a socially-conscious domestic comedy with a little flavour about an undertaker's clerk, Billy Fisher, at odds with his family, unhappily if farcically involved with three girls to whom he is simultaneously engaged, caught in a web of obsessive lies, dreaming of becoming a TV comedian's script-writer.

It is almost consistently funny, it is sensitive, it never stoops to caricature, it succeeds, if you like, in being a sort of *Roots* without Tears.

But too much of what lent depth and force and originality to the book has gone by the board. The episodes have been shuffled and compressed and slotted into three acts and one setting.

I simply cannot understand why the two writers and Mr. Anderson did not choose a more loose-limbed, filmic idiom, and instead plumped for a determinedly naturalistic convention, placing the play within the confines of the Fisher home.*

As a result of this, we lose some of the best characters in the book, e.g. the contemptible Stamp and the two superbly-drawn undertakers, Shadrack and Duxbury, as well as the brilliant scenes in and outside the dance hall, the office, the working men's club.

Were Messrs. Waterhouse, Hall and Anderson afraid of being taunted with expressionism, I wonder? If ever a work called for the epic idiom it is *Billy Liar*.

Never mind. An opportunity has been lost, and we must be grateful for what we are left with, which is still a considerable achievement. The dialogue is mordant and incisive and the acting without a fault.

In Albert Finney, the authors have found the perfect Billy Liar. His articulate 'day-mares', his mime of anguish when his deceptions are revealed, his play with a stick in the darkness of his garden, reveal once more one of the most potent talents we have.

There is not a single false note in the portraits of the father and mother by George A. Cooper and Mona Washbourne (parts which could have descended to the level of caricature in less expert hands), and the three girls are neatly delineated by Ann Beach, Juliet Cook and Jennifer Jayne.

And though I would have liked to have seen more of Stradhoughton, the Northern town which serves as the background for *Billy Liar*, Alan Tagg has supplied an excellent decor of just the right degree of hideousness, complete with cocktail cabinet which plays *There's No Place Like Home* when opened.

To sum up then, a slight disappointment. But most decidedly worthy of your patronage, especially if you haven't read the book.

* Compare the points made on page 95.

C: W. A. DARLINGTON IN *The Daily Telegraph*

Billy Liar has been adapted by Keith Waterhouse and Willis Hall from the former's novel and while it is quite a good play it is a still better vehicle for an actor. It has given Albert Finney, who for some time past has been showing something more than high promise, a chance to show his full quality.

No completer contrast to his spruce Lysander* at Stratford can be imagined than the shambling, ungainly figure he presents as Billy Fisher.

But it is because he has played Lysander (and for that matter, Coriolanus*) that he can allow Billy to show us not merely the outward absurdity of his fantasies, but their inner grandeur.

For instance, at the moment when he imagines himself a soldier at a military funeral, standing with bowed head and rifle reversed while he imitates the sound of bugles playing the Last Post, the actor not merely conveys the emotion which Billy has stirred up in himself, but transmits its momentary sincerity to the audience. That is real acting.

* Lysander is one of the lovers in Shakespeare's *A Midsummer Night's Dream*, and Coriolanus the central character (a Roman warrior) in Shakespeare's play *Coriolanus*.

THE AUTHORS

Both authors were born in Leeds in 1929. They have in common their close connections with the north of England, and also their experience of journalism. This play was the first work on which they collaborated, but since then they have worked together continuously.

WILLIS HALL'S first opportunities for hearing his writing performed came when he was doing his military service in Malaya. There he wrote many scripts for the Chinese Schools Department of Radio Malaya. When he returned to England he started work as a journalist, but soon devoted all his time to playwriting, particularly for radio and television. His radio work included scripts for young listeners, and one serial, *The Royal Astrologers*, he later adapted for school performance (available in the *Kingswood Plays* series, published by Heinemann). A later play for young children, *The Gentle Knight*, has been published by Blackie. Television stimulated his writing of a large number of successful plays, including a triology set in a sea-side resort, which he later adapted for the stage.

It was a commission from an amateur group of actors from Oxford University that led to his most interesting and moving play, *The Long and the Short and the Tall*. This shows a miscellaneous group of soldiers in the Malayan jungle during the Japanese advance on Singapore in 1942. They are faced with an acute problem: should they kill their Japanese prisoner to help their flight from the enemy? Cooped up in a deserted jungle hut, the strain of the situation reveals to us unexpected sides to their characters.

KEITH WATERHOUSE left school at fifteen. He served in the R.A.F. just after the war, and then, after a number of jobs including a short time in an undertaker's office, worked as a reporter in Yorkshire. After four years, he came to Fleet Street, where he contributed to a number of daily papers, including the *Daily Mirror*. Apart from journalism, his first publication was a novel about a group of children, *There is a Happy Land*. This was followed by a second novel *Jubb*, and then *Billy Liar*. This was an immediate success when it was first published in 1959—the same year as Willis Hall's *The Long and the Short and the Tall* was staged in London.

Both authors collaborated in the play *Billy Liar*, which ran for eighteen months the following year. Since then they have written more plays together, a number of film-scripts (including *Whistle Down the Wind*, *A Kind of Loving*, and *Billy Liar* itself), and a revue, *All Things Bright and Beautiful*. They have also used their sharp ear for dialogue in a number of sketches for satirical programmes on television.

The following books by the same authors are well worth reading:

by WILLIS HALL
The Long and the Short and the Tall in *Hereford Plays* series, published by Heinemann
Airmail from Cyprus a television play in *The Television Playwright*, published by Michael Joseph
A Glimpse of the Sea, *Last Day in Dreamland*, and *Return to the Sea* (one volume) published by Evans Brothers

by KEITH WATERHOUSE
There is a Happy Land published by Michael Joseph, Penguin Books and Longmans, Green & Co. Ltd.
Jubb published by Michael Joseph and Penguin Books
Billy Liar, the novel, is published by Michael Joseph, and also available in the *Heritage of Literature* series, published by Longmans, Green & Co. Ltd.

QUESTIONS FOR DISCUSSION

1   What does Billy feel towards Florence, his grandmother? How does her presence in the house affect the family situation?

2   What do we learn about Billy from his store of calendars?

3   Does Billy always realize that he is lying?

4   In many ways Arthur and Billy are very similar, for example they share a number of jokes. In what ways, though, are they different? (The authors' notes on *page 98* will help.)

5   When Arthur reads from Alice's letter: 'We are just ordinary folk', Billy retorts: 'I'm not ordinary folk even if she is' (*page 15, speech 8*). Why does this remark of his mother's annoy him so? What does he mean?

6   When Billy and his father talk together after tea (*page 31*), in what way does Geoffrey's attitude change? Why is it that this new attitude does not last long?

7   'If that's what they learned him at grammar school I'm glad I'm bloody uneducated!' (*page 34, speech 6.*) Is this a fair remark? What does it tell us about Geoffrey?

8   Rita's intrusion into the house is a shock. Alice clearly despises her, saying: 'I've met her type before' (*page 56, speech 6*). What is her type? Do you agree with Alice's impression of Rita?

9   In their production note (*pages 96–9*), the authors say that 'Barbara and Rita . . . should, in fact, be as real as Liz'. Do you think that the characters of the three girls are drawn realistically? Is any one of the girls less like a real person than the other two?

10   Does Billy feel love for any of the three girls?

11   What new impression do we get of Geoffrey's character when he is speaking to his wife about her dead mother (*page 62, speeches 3 and 5*)?

12   The climax to the last scene is Billy's final row with his father (*page 81, speeches 15 and 16*), in which Geoffrey declares: 'You want to be grateful.' With which of them do we sympathize here? Is either of them being reasonable?

13   'I don't know where he'll end up—it's not our fault, I do know that. We've done our best for him' (*page 48, speech 10*). What are your reactions to Alice's remark? How is Billy likely to be on the day after the play takes place? Whose fault, in fact, is it that Billy is 'Billy Liar'?

14   In a review of the first production in the *Evening Standard*, the critic wrote:

> '*Billy Liar* has the outward veneer of a riotous farce and the inner heart of significant comedy.'

To what extent do you agree with this description of the play?

15   The review on *page 105* mentions that the actor who first played the part of Billy was helped by his earlier experience acting two Shakespearian parts. In what ways could this have been a help?

16   What aspects on the play would have been most helped in performance by Alan Tagg's design for the set? (See the drawing on *page 93*, and the review on *page 104*.)